BETTER RESUMES FOR ATTORNEYS & PARALEGALS

BETTER RESUMES FOR ATTORNEYS & PARALEGALS

by
ADELE LEWIS
Former President and Founder
Career Blazers Agency, Inc.

and
DAVID A. SALTMAN,
Esq., J.D., L.L.M.
Partner in the East Windsor, N.J.,
law firm of Newman, Herman, Saltman,
Levitt & Feinson
Member N.J. and Fla. Bar

BARRON'S

BARRON'S EDUCATIONAL SERIES, INC.

To David's wife, Robin, and their children, Kari, Andy, Jason, and Julie, without whom this endeavor would not be possible.

© Copyright 1986 by Barron's Educational Series, Inc.

All inquiries should be addressed to:
Barron's Educational Series, Inc.
250 Wireless Boulevard
Hauppauge, New York 11788

Library of Congress Catalog Card No. 86-3491

International Standard Book No. 0-8120-3649-2

Library of Congress Cataloging-in-Publication Data

Lewis, Adele Beatrice, 1927-
  Better résumés for attorneys and paralegals.

  1. Law—Vocational guidance—United States.
2. Legal assistants—Vocational guidance—United States.
3. Resumés (Employment) I. Saltman, David A.
II. Title.
KF297.Z9L48 1986   650.1′4′02434   86-3491
ISBN 0-8120-3649-2

PRINTED IN THE UNITED STATES OF AMERICA

456   100   98765

Contents

As law becomes more complex and sophisticated, so does the procedure for recruiting and job hunting. There was a time when job seekers could simply visit a law office and be interviewed, but that time has long since passed.

Employers and personnel departments all over the country report that résumés have become the most effective way of screening candidates to determine who will be interviewed. Résumés are expected of applicants for legal positions at every level.

These same employers also indicate that of the thousands of résumés they receive on a daily basis, very few impress them enough to consider their writers as serious employment candidates.

This book will show you, in a logical step-by-step procedure, exactly how to write a superior résumé—one which will strengthen your job campaign and ultimately get you the very position you want.

We wish to thank William Lewis, president of Career Blazers Personnel Services, Inc., for his suggestions and continual support; and Theresa McGee for her understanding and unlimited typing. A special thanks to our editors, Carole Berglie and Ruth Pecan.

Finding the Right Job

Job hunting can be either a catastrophe or a triumph. It can plummet you to the depths of depression or lift you to the summit of self-confidence. From long experience in dealing with a variety of job seekers, we've come to the conclusion that looking for and getting a job is a *skill.* It is a skill that anyone can learn easily, and perhaps for that reason it is too often disregarded or discarded. Like any skill, it requires some training, careful analysis, and huge amounts of determination and perseverance. If you are armed with the right tools for job hunting, finding your "place in the sun" can be an exciting as well as a rewarding experience.

In looking for a job, always aim for the best available and try to avoid settling for less. But you must maintain an open and realistic attitude, evaluating each opportunity with a flexible and farsighted view. Even if at the outset you don't find the "perfect" job, the one you do get may be the first step of your climb to success.

While we believe in trying to hold out for the very best, we are also aware that a job is often what you make of it. It is not unusual to hear that someone who took an associate's job very soon moved into a senior associate's position. Remember that the most exciting jobs are usually filled by people who are already with the firm.

Are Jobs Available?

One of the most important attributes a job seeker must have is a realistic and optimistic point of view. You must realize that, whether the economy is booming or sluggish, there are always job openings. Law firms are forever recruiting. Some people retire, others are promoted, and staff vacancies are created. Usually someone must be hired to fill them. No matter what economic conditions may be, someone is always trying to hire someone else. Were this not so, employment agencies would have to close their doors; on the contrary, more than 5,000 agencies in the United States are currently interviewing applicants and getting job specifications from personnel directors. And they support themselves by the fees they get for matching applicants to the job "specs."

In times of economic recession, recent law graduates might have to hunt a little longer for jobs, liberal arts graduates may have to settle temporarily for lesser goals, and the "phased outs" might have to change specialties or even relocate; but if each person is looking seriously for work and puts forth sincere effort, more than adequate compensation will result. Often, the outcome of a successful job campaign (even in "hard times") is several job offers, and the problem changes from "how to find a job" to "which one shall I accept?"

It is our belief that you should take the job where you'll be happiest. Every job has its psychological fringe benefits, and these, in the long run, can more than counterbalance what might be a slight initial salary deficiency. If you are happy in a job, you will do good work (and conversely, if you do good work, you'll be happy) and rapidly receive tangible recognition. In addition, contentment in your work will spill over into other areas of your life and is, therefore, an important and vital job asset.

The Positive Side

There is always a shortage of job seekers in certain areas. Can you believe that law offices all over the country are reporting their needs for qualified job applicants with two to ten years experience? Although everybody hears about a supposed oversupply of lawyers, the people in a position to hire are conscious of the difficulties in recruiting personnel today. More men and women are graduating with law degrees, but many go on to government jobs or into law-related fields. Other graduates are women who soon leave the profession to raise a family and—at the most—return to work only in a part-time capacity.

At the moment, law offices are faced with serious hiring problems. They report a lack of capable applicants for any position. There may be many people hunting for jobs; there are still many jobs looking for people.

Another reason for this personnel shortage is that employed people are "staying put." Law offices are experiencing less turnover than in the recent past, and no longer are there employed people in search of greener pastures, willing to gamble on "trading-up." Consequently the total number of experienced and qualified people who are job hunting is smaller—much smaller—than in recent years.

It might well be that the type of position you are seeking is much easier to find now than it would have been in the sixties or early seventies. This is the positive aspect of a slow lawyer and paralegal market. There is the pervasive feeling of potential inflation; people who are working are not looking for new or better job opportunities, but rather are seeking stability. This leaves fewer people competing for the existing jobs. As a result, in what would seem to be a tight job market because of the influx of lawyers, it might be far easier than you had expected to find the job you want.

The Nitty Gritty

In the job hunt your single most important tool can easily be a carefully thought-out résumé. Whether or not an interview is granted may result from the impression made by this résumé. In any law office the first contact, and on many occasions the last contact, with a person is through a résumé.

Résumé—pronounced *REHZ-uh-may*—is from a French word meaning "summary." A résumé is not only a summary of your experience and education; it is also an advertisement selling you. Like any advertisement, it should be attractive, well organized, and capable of creating interest in its product—you!

This book will teach you to write a better résumé, a résumé that will get results, that will get the interviews, and that ultimately will get you a better job.

Contents and Style

Every résumé must *identify and describe* the writer. You *must* include the following:

> Your name, address, and telephone number
> Description of your work history
> State licenses
> Publications, if any
> Membership in professional organizations
> Description of your educational background
> Academic honors, if any

You *may* or *may not* include the items below:

> Job objective or career goal
> Brief personal history
> Capsule description of work history
> Hobby information
> Willingness to travel or relocate
> Military service
> Statement of health

You must *never* insert the following details:

> Reasons for leaving past jobs
> Past salaries or present salary requirements
> A photograph of yourself
> Names of spouse or children
> Names and addresses of references

You have several styles to choose from in writing a résumé. Although every résumé should contain a brief, concise summary of your work history and educational background, the style or approach differs in the arrangement of this data. Despite the variations that exist within each of them, basically there are five different résumé styles or approaches:

- Historical or Chronological
- Functional
- Analytical
- Synoptic/Amplified
- Imaginative, Creative, or Informal

We will discuss and evaluate each of these styles and approaches.

As the name implies, this style presents information in chronological succession. It is necessary, however, that the presentation be in *inverse* chronological order, starting with the present or most recent experience and moving backwards in time.

Dates are always included. They can be displayed in a vertical column set apart from the other information, put on a line before the pertinent information, or included as an integral part of each paragraph of your history. Generally, one of the first two is preferred, as most employers like to be able to determine at a glance the dates involved.

Education is treated in the same manner as your employment history. Your most advanced degree is given first, followed, in inverse order, by all other degrees and certificates. Academic honors would be included in this grouping.

If you care to include a job objective, it would be placed at the very beginning, after your name and address, but before your history. All other required or optional information should be placed at the very end.

As a rule, the chronological approach begins with your most recent experience, whether it be work or education. There are special circumstances where this rule should be broken. For instance, if you secured a college degree by working in one field and going to school nights, and are looking for work in the new field that the degree has qualified you for, you would start with your educational history (after your name and address, of course). However, had you gotten the degree for reasons of pride, but want to continue in the same field you were in prior to completing your studies, you would start the chronology with your work history. In short, give prominence to whatever is most descriptive of your talents and abilities. You want to emphasize, from the start, your most salable assets.

The chronological résumé—like any other—should be brief and consist of only one page, if possible. In no event should it exceed two pages. If you feel that your history *demands* three pages, the information you find so fascinating will probably be a complete bore to a reader of your résumé.

We feel that this style of résumé is the most effective, and strongly recommend its use. A survey of such "résumé readers" as personnel people, office managers, and corporate executives confirms our opinion:

> "...much easier to read..." is a quote from the president of a well-known manufacturing firm.

> "I can tell at a glance if the employment history fits our needs," says the general counsel of a major company listed on the stock exchange.

"...precise and to the point..." is the opinion of the vice-president of a large music and record company.

"Not only is the expertise indicated, but we can easily see how long the person's been employed," says the chairman of a national foundation.

Functional Approach

The functional résumé, as you can assume from its name, emphasizes your qualifications and abilities in terms of your job titles and responsibilities. This style of résumé highlights different areas of experience and is arranged with its most significant functions and responsibilities first. Each job title is followed by a brief description of duties and expertise. Dates are not given or, if included, are inconspicuous.

Education is treated in a separate area and, as with the work history, dates are omitted.

We believe, in order to make a functional résumé more effective, a concise chronological history, including dates, should be added. Even though the functional résumé is a perfect vehicle for describing actual talents and areas of achievement, the omission of dates lessens its effectiveness. A résumé without dates is a much weaker résumé and could even become a liability. Listing all dates will subtly reassure the reader that nothing has been deleted and that no periods of time have been unaccounted for deliberately or, at best, overlooked.

The body of information in this résumé is followed and concluded with optional personal data.

The functional résumé is an excellent presentation for those people who have had few jobs—either attorneys or paralegals who have been employed in one or two firms for a considerable length of time, or younger persons who, so far, have had only one job. In such cases a chronological sequence is of less interest than a thorough description of each function or responsibility.

Analytical Approach

The analytical résumé, like the functional, rejects a historical or chronological sequence of employment and educational history, and instead lists in a chronological sequence an analysis of each particular skill. The particular ability is the important facet in this type of résumé.

Your work history and education are fragmented into significant talents and each skill is listed separately. As these skills have been exercised, probably in more than one position, names of employers and dates are not attached to each item.

The analytical résumé is especially useful when attempting to change career goals. If your qualifications and responsibilities are valuable in more than one field, it is more sensible to emphasize the skill by setting it apart than to bury it with less significant skills.

Like the functional résumé, the usual format for the analytical résumé omits dates. However, most résumé readers feel that a résumé loses effectiveness if dates are not shown. Dateless résumés might imply a spotty work history, involving too many job changes or time gaps that the applicant feels would be awkward to explain. Consequently, we recommend that a very concise chronological history listing all employers, job titles, schools, and dates also be included. This history should be placed right after the job objective, if it is used, or toward the end, immediately before your personal data.

Synoptic/Amplified Approach

The synoptic/amplified résumé is the only style whose organization requires two pages. The first page would consist of your name and address, job objective, chronological history of employment and education, and personal data. The chronological history of employment would list job title and employer, clearly setting off the dates.

At the bottom of the page, in parentheses, would be the statement "Please see following for amplification." The amplification should be limited to one page, but it may be necessary to continue to a second for a total of three pages. The amplification would again list dates of employment and name of employer, as well as your duties and responsibilities in that office.

While this is an effective presentation, especially for a person whose duties and responsibilities went far beyond those normally seen as the functions of a given job title, it has the disadvantage of being one page longer, through its design, than other résumé styles giving the same information. In addition, in preparing the amplification, more space being available, there is a tendency for one to become long-winded and give extraneous information that is not pertinent to the résumé.

Imagination or Creative Approach

A résumé can be as creative as its writer desires. There are, however, three provisos: first, it should contain all the necessary information; second, the information should be easily extracted; and third, it should not be capable of offending anyone.

If you decide to use the creative approach, keep in mind that, while it can serve as a vehicle for displaying your literary or artistic talents, it is primarily a means of communicating certain information which the résumé reader must have. You very well may be a second James

Joyce, but the résumé reader cannot devote his lifetime to your résumé. Similarly, two cartoon characters giving questions and answers might convey all the information and also show your drawing ability, but, while you might make an impression for originality, your résumé might not be read to the end. Keep in mind that if you have published writings you can always indicate on your résumé that you have a list available. It is dangerous to be too gimmicky or too cute. Overly creative résumés might catch the eye. Nevertheless, they often fail to sustain interest, and become completely ineffectual. Most résumé readers feel that a résumé is a business matter and should be presented in a businesslike manner.

If you want to be imaginative, it is best to use some simple device that will distinguish your résumé from the dozens of others that arrive in a law office every day. For instance, you could use colored paper, preferably of a pale or pastel hue soft enough to allow contrast with the printed text. Purple ink on hot pink paper may catch the eye but it also will tire the sight.

Another simple device that makes a résumé stand out is to use different type faces and type sizes for the various parts of the résumé. But the same caveat applies as the use of color: avoid any type that is difficult to read. Also, don't overdo it.

As a general rule, creative résumés may be appropriate to the arts, graphics, and advertising fields; but for the professions, it is best to employ one of the standard résumé styles.

Putting Yourself on Paper

3

When writing your résumé, always remember that its purpose is to make you interesting enough to a potential employer to secure you an interview. Your résumé should be considered as an advertisement for yourself and, like a good ad, it should be visually attractive, brief, and informative. Above all, it should create interest in its product. In this case, *you* are the product.

Who Are You? Identify Yourself

Always start with your name, address, and telephone number in a conspicuous position. If your résumé is longer than one page, be sure that your name is placed conspicuously on every page.

TIP: *Start with your name.*

It is amazing that people would actually go to the trouble of organizing, writing, and having a résumé printed, and then fail to include the essential information that identifies them. We don't know how people can do that, but they do. It happens almost every day.

Of course, Adele's employment agency receives many résumés as part of someone's direct mail campaign, but most are in response to ads they have run in the newspapers. One of her clients, a major law firm, once asked her to recruit an attorney who not only had experience and background in real estate and property taxes, but was also a CPA. She put an ad in the classified columns and received more than forty résumés in reply. Of the forty, only one met the precise requirements. It was well organized and well presented and had only three deficiencies: it lacked a name, an address, and a phone number. You can be sure that this was not the first time, nor will it be the last time, that such an omission kept a job seeker from a job that fitted perfectly.

How Long?

If there is one single cardinal rule in writing a résumé, it is this: *Keep it brief!*

TIP: *Be concise and to the point.*

No matter how superior a work history you might have, do your utmost to consolidate it into *one,* or at the very most, *two* pages. Our survey showed that all résumé readers concur in a preference for a concise résumé—not more than two pages. These are some of the comments we received:

> A personnel manager: "I read about fifty résumés a day and *never* go beyond the second page."

> An electronics executive: "I want facts and only the ones I need for a judgment."

> A book publisher: "If it's more than three pages, I assume it's an autobiographical manuscript and send it to a junior reader."

> A partner in a law firm says: "If the applicant tells me he is expert in probate law, that is all he needs to say on his résumé; I don't need to be told that he knows how to file a will or contest one."

Job Objective or Career Goal

Even though the statement of a job objective is frequently advised in a résumé, a recent survey indicates that its inclusion is optional, as most employers are indifferent to its use. If it is stated, it should be placed right after the initial identifying data (name, address, and phone number).

*TIP: **Connect the job objective with the rest of the information.***

The job objective should be brief—one or two lines—and your goal should be justified by the educational and work experience that will follow it.

You should avoid stating an objective that is too confining; you do not want one that will cancel out opportunities you might be interested in. On the other hand, avoid the use of clichés—"A challenging position where I can meet people"—or overly vague generalities —"A job that will interest me and stimulate my best efforts."

Often the job objective can be replaced by a capsule résumé. Not only is the capsule résumé more informative and more interesting to the reader, but it is more likely to have an efficacious result. And that is what you expect from every element of your résumé.

Capsule Résumé

A capsule résumé is a summary in three or four lines of the most pertinent information contained in your résumé. It is the best way of emphasizing a solid work background and of highlighting qualifications appropriate to a specific job opening. While it often involves retyping the résumé, the capsule résumé is a means of directing it to a very concrete offer of employment without having to reorganize the résumé completely.

TIP: A capsule résumé highlights your marketable features.

Consider a hypothetical case. A man has worked fifteen years as a negligence lawyer as well as a matrimonial attorney. His general capsule résumé would read:

> 15 years' experience in the field of trial work

but in answering an ad for a litigation attorney, he would have:

> 15 years' experience in litigation including extensive experience in negligence and matrimonial work

The capsule résumé, if used, should follow your name and address and serve as a headline for the body of your résumé.

Basic Information

The body of your résumé should contain a brief history of your work experience and a concise summary of your education. You can start with either one of the two, but we believe it is best to place the most marketable information first. An experienced person usually starts with the work history, but a newcomer to the job market, with little more than summer or part-time work behind him, would be wiser to begin with an educational summary.

TIP: If you've had experience, start with your work history, but if you've just graduated from law school or paralegal school, start with your educational background.

EDUCATIONAL HISTORY: COLLEGE AND/OR ADVANCED DEGREE

Your education, like your work history, is arranged in an inverse chronological order. Begin with your most advanced, or most recent, educational experience, and work backwards until you reach your bachelor's degree. If you have already had significant work experience, simply give the date, the degree, and the name of your school.

TIP: List your most advanced or most significant degree first.

If you are a college graduate, it stands to reason that you finished high school, so it is not necessary to list it. If your high school or preparatory school is very prestigious, however, naming it may enhance your prospects in certain fields of employment. On the other hand, it may be considered snobbishness on your part and work to your detriment.

TIP: *List all dates.*

Be sure to list all dates of attendance at college as well as date of graduation and the degree received. A recent graduate should include the major and minor study sequences, as well as any academic honors that were earned. If you maintained a high scholastic average (three or four points out of a possible four), you should mention your academic standing. Don't call attention to a mediocre average by mentioning it in your résumé. Of course, any merit scholarships or fellowships should be mentioned.

TIP: *Extracurricular activity can be important.*

If you are a recent graduate, you should list all of your extracurricular activities. Not only does such a list paint a more rounded portrait, but it also indicates talents that are outside of your work experience or areas of study. Membership in your college debating society implies an articulate, poised personality. A class officer will be pictured as an outgoing individual with leadership potential. A staff member of a college publication would usually be seen as appealing.

TIP: *Recent graduates should mention summer or part-time employment.*

Recent graduates should list all of their summer and part-time jobs, even if they have no relationship with present job goals. This experience should, like any other, include names of employers, dates, job titles, and duties. Simply showing that you have worked before is significant to a prospective employer. Experience as a clerk-typist, waiter, babysitter, or anything else will demonstrate an already proven ability and willingness to work. A part-time history establishes the applicant's preparedness to accept responsibility.

PROFESSIONAL SOCIETIES AND PUBLICATIONS

List all professional associations and organizations that have a bearing on your career goals. Membership in job-related organizations implies dedication to your field of work and an ability to get along with others. For example:

> Member, Legal Aid Society; member Student Bar Association; Phi Beta Kappa.

List titles of all publications and note when and where they were published. If the list is extensive, merely highlight it and offer a complete list if wanted.

> Published in American Bar Association Journal and the State Bar Journal. List of publications furnished on request.

ARRANGING YOUR EMPLOYMENT HISTORY

Begin with your present or most recent employment and then work backwards in an inverted chronological order. In this manner, the most important information, which is usually the most recent, is emphasized.

TIP: *Start with your present or most recent experience and work back.*

Each entry should include the name and address of the employer, the dates involved, the job title, and a brief description of your responsibilities. The description should be succinct and to the point, but should still include all basic activities of each particular job. Use implied pronouns and clear, simple language.

TIP: *Avoid the third person (he or she). Don't overuse the pronoun "I."*

Writing in the third person is stylistically objectionable. Overuse of "I" is redundant—the person reading the résumé knows you are the subject of your own résumé. For example, don't write:

<blockquote>
He supervised a staff of twenty,
</blockquote>

or

<blockquote>
I supervised a staff of twenty,
</blockquote>

but instead:

<blockquote>
Supervised staff of twenty.
</blockquote>

Using implied pronouns avoids an impression of boastfulness on the one hand and, on the other, it gives your résumé a brisk, businesslike air which results in a more professional impression.

Nonetheless, even though you want to strive for brevity in your résumé, avoid the use of abbreviations except in listing your university or professional degrees, such as B.A., J.S.D., J.D. or L.L.M. Also be sure that all dates are correct, providing an unbroken sequence, and that there are no spelling or grammatical errors.

PERSONAL DATA

Personal data may be included, at your option, in order to provide a more fully rounded picture of you as an individual. This section, by definition, should contain material *pertinent* to the job seeker and his or her qualifications.

However, Adele's agency has actually received résumés that included the job seeker's glove size (the person was *not* looking for a job as a glove model), parents' birthdays, pets' names, and monthly rent and electrical bill. Inclusion of this type of information is not only considered verbose; it's in very poor taste.

TIP: *Keep personal data to the minimum—and be honest.*

Information concerning your age, marital status, number of children, height and weight can be included, but this is strictly optional. You might want to include your height and weight in order to give a more three-dimensional picture of yourself. However, if you are overweight—please try to lose weight!

It *is* true that overweight people have more difficulty in finding a job than those who are slim. It's not only a question of appearance; it has to do with the policy of many companies which require a physical examination before making a job offer. Being overweight is considered a health hazard, and many employers are sensitive to this. We once referred a very well qualified, but 30 pounds overweight, attorney to a Wall Street firm. He was offered the job if he would *promise* to lose weight. He is still on the job—though 25 pounds lighter. However, be particularly careful that if you do carry a few extra pounds and you do mention your weight, *tell it as it is!* When you go for the interview, your slight deviation from the truth will be obvious, embarrassing, and might even cost you the job. Being caught in a lie is usually the kiss of death.

Because of recent equal employment acts (especially the Equal Employment Opportunity Act of 1972), it has been illegal for any employer to discriminate because of age, sex, or national origin. Employers have been very conscientious about adhering to this. Regarding age, many companies are relearning what they had forgotten as our culture became more youth oriented: that the experience and wisdom that come with maturity are major assets. Therefore, since your age is not allowed to be a factor in your opportunity for employment, it is strictly up to you whether to include it in your résumé. If you decide to include it, put down your date of birth rather than your current age. Not only is it more professional, but you won't have to update this on your résumé should you later decide to change jobs: you would just have to add information about your current employment. Of course, be completely honest as to your age.

TIP: *Marital status need not be mentioned.*

Marital status is completely optional. Since marital status has absolutely nothing to do with your job qualifications, it really isn't necessary to include such information in your résumé. Keep in mind that according to the Equal Employment Opportunity act, it is against the law to discriminate because of marital status. Remember, we said before that the *only* information *necessary* to include is that which describes your educational and work history.

Many people feel that saying they are married, with children, implies a greater sense of responsibility and hence, more stability. This is not necessarily true. Jobs that require a lot of overtime or travel are often filled more successfully by unmarried people who can be more flexible. Including this personal information is up to you, so consider whether it will be an advantage in getting the position.

HOBBIES AND LEISURE ACTIVITIES

Should you include hobbies and leisure-time activities? You must decide for yourself. If you feel that a description of your avocations will enhance your image, by all means include them.

TIP: List only those hobbies and activities that can help to describe you.

A 55-year-old man who participates in outdoor sports should say that he's a sailing enthusiast. This helps the reader of his résumé to regard him as a healthy and active person. After all, despite the jokes about Gerald Ford's falling on the ski slope, he was engaging in a sport that is usually considered an activity for someone thirty years younger. Think also of Ronald Reagan, another active man who exercises regularly and rides horses on his ranch. Telling your prospective employer that you are active in a vigorous sport is a way of letting him or her know that you are in good health and also a good sport.

An indication that you play chess could be of interest on your résumé if you were looking for legal writing work or real estate work. It would show that you have patience for details and an ability to concentrate. A lawyer we know was granted an interview by a small, attractive law firm because of his table tennis championships; the prospective employer wanted to see what a table tennis champion looked like!

If you include your hobbies on your résumé, there are two things you must remember. First, keep it brief! You don't want to create the impression that all of your time and energy is spent on your hobbies or that you are unable to sustain an interest in one or two avocations and need dozens to fight off boredom. Second, be completely honest! Don't put down orchid-growing or gliding because you feel that they are exotic and will make you appear more interesting. They are liable to make you so interesting to the interviewer that things will start off with a discussion of the strange coincidence that the two of you share a common interest in such an esoteric hobby!

MILITARY SERVICE

Completion of military service is of interest to any employer in times of universal conscription. Completion of that service, or a draft-deferred status, should be mentioned on the résumé as a means of assuring the employer that you have an initial intention of being a permanent employee. The draft is not in effect right now, however, and the completion of military service would be of minimal interest to most employers.

Another reason would arise from your military service having a direct effect on your job capabilities. If you had received special training in the service and your nonmilitary specialty resulted from that training, both of those facts should be mentioned along with relevant dates and the highest rank achieved.

TIP: Mention your military service so that there is no time lapse in your history.

If your military service has no relevance to your intended work area, it would be best to simply state that you completed military service and were honorably discharged. You could add arm and branch of service if you desire. If you are beyond draft age, there is no point in elaborating on military service unless it adds important occupational information to your résumé.

PERSONAL HISTORY

A short paragraph describing your personal background can be included if you feel that it would offer information not readily discernable from your work or education but which would add to your marketability. Our survey showed that very few résumé readers feel that it should be included. Most agree that, with only the rarest exceptions, all pertinent information is already included in the résumé.

TIP: Use personal history only if it makes you more employable.

Some examples that could be appropriate are:

> Born in Spain of American father and Spanish mother. Came to U.S. at age five. Returned to Spain with mother every summer. Speak, read, write Spanish as fluently as English.

Or take the case of a recent college graduate whose résumé indicated no work experience at all, not even part-time or summer jobs. Her personal history indicated, nonetheless, that she had not been the least bit idle:

> Oldest of four children. Due to mother's death, have managed household and supervised younger siblings since age fourteen.

Observe that in the first instance, the information offered was valuable to an employer in that it not only claimed fluency in Spanish but corroborated the claim. In the second instance, a responsibility and maturity which belied the lack of work experience was manifested. These are valuable pieces of information; the fact that you were born and raised on Sutton Place or in Bronxville, or that you spent your summers in Bar Harbor and winters in Marbella is not.

LOOK AT ME NOW!

Some people seem to think it is a good idea to include a picture of themselves with the résumé. We have found that most résumé readers react very strongly *against* applicants who enclose photographs.

One personnel director told us, "When I see a photograph, I don't bother reading the résumé. I figure any person counting on looks doesn't have much else to sell."

TIP: Don't include your photograph.

A partner in one of the Big Eight firms said, "There are businesses where the employer would like to know what an applicant looks like—some are even legitimate—but ours isn't one of them."

So—while including a photo is not completely taboo, we strongly advise against doing it. It is worth noting that if an offer of employment were to request a résumé *and* a photo, unless it were in the modeling or entertainment fields, it could be considered illegal on grounds that this is a covert form of racial screening. In addition, such a request may indicate that the job has duties other than those normally pertaining to the position offered.

PERSONAL REFERENCES

You should never supply the names of your references in your résumé. Not only is it unprofessional, but it can also cause unnecessary bother to the references listed. You should only give permission to call your references when an employer has indicated that he is really interested in someone with your qualifications.

TIP: Don't list references.

Always, of course, get permission from all parties involved to use them as references before releasing their names. Be sure, also, that your references can be reached quickly. List people who can be reached by phone rather than by mail. If giving the business phone of a reference, always ascertain that they are still employed by that company.

If your name has changed through marriage or for any other reason during your work or educational history, be sure that your references know you by your new name. It is wise for married women to indicate their maiden as well as married names on the résumé, if the change occurred during any of the résumé history.

REASONS FOR LEAVING PAST JOBS

Your résumé should be a brief summary of your own particular talents, abilities, and qualifications. Since the reasons that you have left previous employment do not add to that summary, they should not be included in your résumé. Like salary requirements, your reasons for having left earlier jobs should be discussed in the interview.

TIP: *Don't tell why you left previous jobs.*

THE BUSINESS OF MONEY

Never discuss salary in your résumé — neither minimum salary requirements nor your earnings in the past.

TIP: *Never mention salaries.*

Most employers consider salary a most confidential subject. Your résumé will probably be seen by many people in the company who would not be entitled to know your rate of pay, so no indications of it should appear in your résumé. You will have an opportunity to discuss it in the interview. The interviewer should be the one to introduce the subject, and almost certainly will.

TRUTH WILL OUT

Despite our having discussed it earlier, we feel that we cannot over-emphasize the necessity of being truthful in all elements of your résumé. It is probable that many lies, half-truths, distortions, or exaggerations will escape detection in an interview. It is even possible that you can get your immediate supervisor in a previous job to back you up. Eventually, however, you will be put to the test and will find that you have not only lost the job, but seriously damaged your prospects for future employment.

TIP: *Honesty is the best policy.*

Often a recently graduated student, having prepared a résumé, will feel that it is stark and bare and needs "beefing up." Suddenly, it becomes the résumé of a student who completed a law degree in 2½ years, while holding down a job as a newspaper photographer, editing the college newspaper, working on the staff of the yearbook, holding class office, and graduating with an "A" average. Rather than being astonished by the energy and drive, most résumé readers would shake their heads, and thinking, "This kid has too much biography," throw the résumé into the wastebasket.

Admittedly, there are successful people who bluffed — which is a polite way of saying "lied" — their ways into the positions that started them up the ladder, but you can be assured that there were very few who were able to do so, and many who tried and were found out.

Looking Good!

4

Since your résumé probably will be the first contact between you and your prospective employer, it is imperative that it invite reading. The physical appearance of your résumé is as important as the information it contains. A résumé that is hard to read or confusing to interpret will end up in the wastebasket, while the reader goes on to the next one. Your résumé is competing with many others and as a result is scanned very rapidly. (Our inquiries have shown that offices rarely give more than 30 seconds of attention to a résumé in order to decide if it merits a detailed reading.) The more attractive your résumé is, the better impression it will make in the few moments that are given it initially.

> **TIP:** *Your résumé should appeal to the eye.*

Bearing in mind that your résumé is meant to serve, in part, as a personal advertisement, take a hint from the professional ad-makers. As one "pro" expressed it, "A good ad *looks* good enough to grab your attention, and once it's got it, *tells* you what it wants to say as quickly and effectively as it can." Like the ad, your résumé should be visually compelling and to the point.

Cure Your Logorrhea!

Don't run off at the mouth — or, rather, the typewriter. *Keep it brief!* We've already said that, but it can bear repetition because it is important. One page, if possible (and do everything to make it possible); two pages, if necessary.

> **TIP:** *Keep your résumé brief.*

Remember that you are striving for one of two pages. Your résumé should contain just enough information to sketch your abilities and qualifications. It is not an autobiography nor a vehicle for your personal philosophy. Your aim is not to tell the reader all about yourself, but to create enough interest so that the reader will want to know more about you.

Grab the Eye!

The first thing you have to consider before typing the résumé is the layout of the copy. Whether you use one of the samples we will give you or create your own, be sure that the total effect is pleasing to the eye. But be equally sure that it is easy to read and that the different sections are clearly separate from one another.

TIP: *Have adequate margins.*

Use your ground — the white space on the paper — effectively, even using your margins imaginatively. We have received many résumés whose information indicated easily placed applicants, but that were so badly laid-out and cluttered that we were hesitant about sending them on to prospective employers. (Note, for example, on our suggested layouts and sample résumés, that there are always at least two spaces between every block of information.)

TIP: *Use standard-size, good-quality paper.*

Even though odd-sized paper might be visually arresting, it can create a filing problem. Use the standard 8½″ x 11″ paper. It is easily filed and easily handled.

Choose a good-quality watermarked bond paper and, if not using white, be sure it is a pale color that will contrast well with the color of the type. Use only one side of the paper, and if the résumé is more than one page, staple the pages together, being sure that your name appears on each page.

TIP: *Proofread your résumé.*

Be sure that there are no spelling or typing errors. It is a good idea to have several people proofread your résumé for you. In addition, unless you are a superlative typist (or plan to have your résumé printed with the printer's own type), it is worth the small expense to have a professional type it for you. If you do so, it would be to your further advantage to find a typist or service which has either a word processor or an IBM Selectric with different fonts to have your résumé laid out with distinctive type faces or section titles.

Reproducing Your Résumé

Once employers expected every résumé they received to be typed individually; fortunately, those days have passed. Although carbon copies (because of smudging and lack of clarity) are not acceptable, any other duplicating process which turns out clean, sharp copies may be used.

TIP: *Each copy of your résumé does not have to be individually typed.*

Mimeographing, photocopying, offset printing, and multilith processing all give excellent results. Even Xerox copies are acceptable as long as they are sharp and clear. It goes without saying that if you want to spend the money to have your résumé printed from set type, that too would be acceptable.

As the success of your job campaign very likely may hinge upon the appearance of your résumé, it is important you choose a service that turns out a professional-looking product. These services are listed in the Yellow Pages under the heading "Offset Reproductions." Many of them will be able to assist you with the layout and a choice of available type faces.

TIP: Use a good-quality paper.

It is important that your résumé be reproduced on a good quality paper. If you are having a typescript reproduced, it is best to insist upon a good-quality watermarked bond. If it is to be printed, an equally fine opaque paper should be used. Don't be afraid of the additional expense of a quality paper; it will add little to the total cost, and the effect it creates is well worth it.

Sample Résumés

5

On the following pages you will find samples of what we consider to be "job-getting" résumés. Although these represent a variety of fields and a diversification of job categories, you will find they all have several factors in common.

Each résumé is attractively laid out. The important facts and dates are stated simply and clearly. The information contained is consolidated into a reverse chronological history.

If you study the résumés in this section, you will find they all contain the *vital information* as described on page 4. (Note the information that must be included.) Some contain such *optional information* as "job or career objective" while others may include choices of hobbies or personal histories. Note also that *none* of these résumés includes such information as reasons for leaving past jobs or past, present or expected salaries.

As you review these sample résumés, keep in mind what we discussed earlier. You will soon get the feel of a *better résumé* and will find that writing your own will follow easily.

ATTORNEYS

LAURA SUE CARTER
236 West Street
Hendersville, Tennessee 37305
(615) 971-6666

OBJECTIVE: To secure a position as a Summer Associate with an aggressive law firm.

EDUCATION: **University of Alabama College of Law**
Selma, Alabama
Will graduate June 1987

Honors and
Activities: Team Member--Senator Robert Jones Labor
Law Moot Court. Competition in New York
in March 1987.

Moot Court Board member

Chairperson, Moot Court Board Problem Committee

Legal Clinic, Criminal Advocacy, spring 1986

Dean's List, winter and fall 1985 and 1986

Northwestern University
Chicago, Illinois
B.A., June 1984
English major

Honors and
Activities: Dean's List, all semesters
Member National Political Science Honor Society
Member National English Honor Society

PUBLICATIONS
AND REFERENCES: Upon request.

CONSTANCE ANITA KRAVITS

456 Ocean Drive
Los Angeles, California 90005
(213) 738-6767

EDUCATION: Southwestern University School of Law
                              Los Angeles, California
                              J.D. (to be received in 1987)

                              Canisius College
                              Buffalo, New York
                              B.A., June 1984

                              Business major
                              Summa Cum Laude
                              History honors program
                              Pre-law Society
                              Psychology and History Clubs

EMPLOYMENT:

Summer 1985   Moot, Greystone & River, P.C.
                              Los Angeles, California

                              Summer Associate - assisted in preparation
                              of briefs, general claims.

Summer 1984   William A. Robbins, Esq.
                              Long Beach, California

                              Summer Intern - general clerical duties and
                              some paralegal work.

REFERENCES: Available upon request.

MILLARD POLLOCK
1428 Cornelia Drive
Los Angeles, California 90042

Home (213) 671-2236
Work (213) 655-4938

POSITION SOUGHT:

Associate Attorney

EDUCATION:

Stanford University School of Law
J.D., June 1986

Associate Editor, Stanford Law Review (1985-1986)

Pomona College
A.B. in Economics, June 1981

Dean's List, 1979-1981
Stanford Daily News, freelance contributor, 1978-1981

EXPERIENCE:
May 1981 to
December 1983

Sawyer and Sawyer
Los Angeles, California
Law Clerk

Summer 1980

Stanford Hall Legal Services Clinic
Stanford, California
Assistant

REFERENCES:

Furnished upon request.

Patrick J. O'Mara
45 Hunter Lane
New Rochelle, N.Y. 10824

(914) 555-1212

Education:

Columbia University School of Law, New York, N.Y.
Juris Doctor Degree awarded May 1985
Grade Average: Very Good/Good
    Charles Evans Hughes Fellow
    Student Clerk to Honorable Judge Morris E. Lasker - SDNY
    Columbia Human Rights Law Review - Member of the
    Editorial Board and Associate Editor
Participant - Harlan Kiske Stone Honor Competition
Member of the Columbia Society of International Law
First-Year Student Advisor

Concordia University, Montreal, Canada
Bachelor of Arts, Psychology, 1982

Dawson College, Montreal, Canada
Diplome d'Etudes Collegiales (B.A. Prerequisite), 1979

Legal
Experience:

Sept. 1984-   Donald M. Book, Esq., New York, N.Y.
May 1985   Research Assistant -- Collaborate in the research and
       development of a law-related course to be offered
       in the Columbia University School of Public Law.

Summer 1984   Lake and Wood, Esqs., New York, N.Y.
            Summer Associate -- Prepared interrogatories, motions,
       affidavits, and legal memoranda; participated in
       client conferences; did extensive research and writing.

Summer 1983   American Civil Liberties Union, New York, N.Y.
            Legal Intern -- Did extensive research and writing on
       constitutional and Title VII issues; assisted at
       depositions and in trial preparation.

Special
Skills: Speak Spanish and French

Interests: Photography, Swimming, and Tennis

REFERENCES AVAILABLE ON REQUEST

Maryann O'Connor
14 Bennington Drive
Burlington, VT. 05401
(802) 517-1414

EXPERIENCE:

Summer 1985   *Laverne, Bell and Howe*
Lake Hiawatha, Vt.
Summer Associate
Responsibilities included interviewing clients; drafting complaints and employment contracts.

Summer 1984   *Lang and Hoffman, P.C.*
New York, N.Y.
Law Clerk
Responsibilities included drafting briefs, motions, and complaints. Primarily involved in Products Liability, Warranties, and Secured Transactions.

March 1983
to September 1983   *Kenneth Kesselton, Esquire*
Albany, N.Y.
Researcher
Handled Recovery for Personal Injury as a Third Party Beneficiary of a Contract; Motions.

September 1982
to March 1983   *Richard Katz, Esquire*
New York, N.Y.
Researcher
Handled Substantial Performance, Subcontractor's Liens and Bonds, Attorney's Fees.

June 1982
to September 1982   *T. R. Blum & Co.*
New York, N.Y.
Assistant Manager, Jewelry Dept.
Managed the entire department for 3 months. Primarily responsible for ordering, inventory, and selling. Avg. $18,000 per month in sales.

EDUCATION: Seton Hall University School of Law
Newark, N.J.
Visiting Student, Spring 1985

University of Vermont
Burlington, Vt.
Candidate of Juris Doctor, June 1986
Vermont Law Journal, Member, 1984-1986
Moot Court, Regionals: Oralist and Brief Writer, 1984
International Law Society: President, 1985

(continued)

Colorado College
Colorado Springs, Colorado
September 1978 to June 1982
Bachelor of Arts
Major: Sociology

PUBLICATIONS: Comment, *Tort Immunity in Vermont,*
10 Vermont Law Journal #3

REFERENCES FURNISHED UPON REQUEST.

ROBERT CALDWELL

35 Lyndon Way
Macon, Georgia   31207
(912) 744-2666

EDUCATIONAL BACKGROUND:

Mercer University, Walter F. George School
of Law
Macon, Georgia
J.D. Degree, June 1986

- Law Review
- Moot Court Board
- Highest grade Torts
- Highest grade Contracts

University of Arkansas
Little Rock, Arkansas
B.A., May 1977

- Psychology Major
- President, Phi Delta Fraternity

EMPLOYMENT:

Summer 1985

Cohen, Smith & Jones
Little Rock, Arkansas

Law Clerk.   Duties involved general research for preparation of pleadings, including complaints, answered interrogatories, affidavits, and motions.

May 1983/ Sept. 1983

United States Government
Postal Department
Little Rock, Arkansas

Summer employment as a mail carrier and postal clerk.

MILITARY SERVICE:

June 1977/ May 1983

United States Air Force Pilot
Attained rank of Major

REFERENCES:

Available upon request

William A. Elliott
20 Jerome Drive
Putnam Lake
Paterson, New Jersey 08054   Home: (201) 442-0700

PROFESSIONAL
EXPERIENCE:

June 1986   Lewis and Lewis, Esqs.
to present   Tottenville, New York

                       LAW CLERK. Draft state and federal
                       pleadings, mortgages, contracts, trusts,
                       wills, leases, separation agreements,
                       interrogatories; research and appellate
                       brief writing.

EDUCATION: Seton Hall University School of Law
                       Newark, New Jersey
                       J.D., June 1986

                       Newark State College
                       Union, New Jersey
                       B.A., History, 1982

                       Dean's List, 1979-1982
                       Editor of College newspaper, 1980-1982
                       Student Delegate to the Consortium of
                         East Jersey, an intercollegiate
                         educational consortium.

References and writing samples furnished upon request.

Gregory L. Charles
78 Oaktree Drive
Camden, New Jersey 18100

(609) 268-1978

EMPLOYMENT:

December 1984–   Neighborhood Legal Services Association
September 1986   Trenton, New Jersey

                          LAW CLERK
                          Interview clients and maintain a case load,
                          represent clients at unemployment compensation
                          and social security disability hearings,
                          research issues and write memoranda for the
                          use of staff attorneys.

Summer 1984   Susquehanna Legal Services
                          Bloomsburg, Pennsylvania

                          LAW CLERK
                          Duties included research, writing both informal
                          memoranda and formal briefs.

Summer 1982   Dun and Muhlenberg
                          New Haven, Connecticut

                          LAW CLERK
                          General clerking duties.

EDUCATION: Northwestern University School of Law
                          Chicago, Illinois
                          J.D. Degree, June 1985

                          University of Michigan
                          Ann Arbor, Michigan
                          B.A., Business, May 1982

ADMISSIONS: Admitted to New Jersey Bar, June 1986
                          Admitted to Michigan Bar, November 1985

REFERENCES: Available upon request.

ELLEN A. BROZOWSKI
81 St. Marks Place
Teaneck, New Jersey 07665

(201) 221-7543

EMPLOYMENT

February 1983
to present

Revlon and Martin, Esqs.
East Windsor, N.J.

Law Clerk. Duties include depositions, motions,
interviewing clients, and research.

September 1981
to January 1983

Carr and Victor, Esqs.
Lawrenceville, N.J.

Law Clerk. Duties included real estate, motions,
and research.

Summer 1980

Mercer County Department of Law
Trenton, N.J.

Legal Assistant. General duties included motion work
and civil commitment hearings.

EDUCATION:

University of Miami School of Law
J.D., June 1981

Two terms on Dean's List
Finalist in first-year Moot Court competition
1979-1980 National Mock Trial competition
1980 state client counseling competition

Northwestern University
B.A., Political Science, June 1978

Dean's List, 1975-1978

AFFILIATIONS:

Mercer County Bar Association
New Jersey State Bar Association
Admitted to practice before District Court for New Jersey
Pool attorney for office of the Public Defender, Mercer
  Trial Region
Member of Volunteer Lawyers Project of Mercer County Legal
  Aid Society
Successful candidate for State Bar of Pennsylvania

REFERENCES: Available upon request

PABLO GONZALEZ
12 Prickly Pear Road
Durham, North Carolina 27707

(919) 683-6833

EXPERIENCE

June 1979
to present

Chambers and Alston, Esquires
Durham, North Carolina

Attorney
Responsible for preparing depositions,
memoranda; interview clients, prepare
research reports.

June 1978
to June 1979

Durson and Durson, P.C.
Durham, North Carolina

Law clerk
Duties included research for mortgages,
contracts, and trusts.

EDUCATION

Villanova University
Philadelphia, Pennsylvania
J.D., June 1978

*Villanova Law Quarterly, editor, 1977-1978;
  staff member, 1976-1977

Rutgers University
Camden, New Jersey
B.A., June 1975. Major in Sociology

*Dean's List, 1972-1975
*Member Pre-Law Society
*Member Sociology Club

PUBLICATIONS
AND
REFERENCES

Available upon request

Stephen Phillips
4500 Clarksburg Road
Philadelphia, Pennsylvania 19106
(215) 671-2573

EXPERIENCE
1984-Present

Interstate Commerce Commission, Philadelphia Office of the General Counsel

Litigation Attorney. Responsible for representing the Commission and the United States whenever the agency's actions are challenged in court, and for advising the Commission regarding the legality of its programs and actions.

Summer 1983

Smith and Jones, Boston

Summer Associate. General business litigation in securities, tax, and corporate proceedings.

Summer 1982

McGee and Newman, Washington, D.C.

Law Clerk. Duties included research and drafting of memoranda of law.

EDUCATION

Rutgers University School of Law, Newark, New Jersey
Awarded Juris Doctor, June 1984

Selected to participate in Prize Moot Court Competition based on performance in Moot Court Competition.

Wharton School and College of Liberal Arts and Sciences, University of Pennsylvania, Philadelphia
Awarded B.S. in Economics (major in Accounting), June 1981

Beta Alpha Psi, the National Accounting Honor Society.

PROFESSIONAL ASSOCIATIONS

Member of the Bar of the State of New York, New Jersey, and Pennsylvania

Admitted to practice before the United States Supreme Court, the United States Courts of Appeals for the District of Columbia, Fifth, Tenth, and Eleventh Circuits, and the United States District Courts for the Southern and Eastern Districts of New York

American Bar Association

New York State Bar Association

REFERENCES

Available upon request

Michael M. Danko
1233 Raven Park Avenue
Glencoe, Illinois 60022
(312) 971-5656

EMPLOYMENT

**May 1984
to present**

Mitchell and Kern   Chicago, Illinois
ATTORNEY

(40-lawyer litigation firm)

Write briefs, take depositions, argue motions, attend pretrial conferences, and try minor jury cases. Specialize in "working up" defense of drug liability lawsuits.

**February 1981
to April 1984**

Newton Laboratories   North Chicago, Illinois
ATTORNEY

(Developer, manufacturer, and distributor of human health care products including hospital products, medical devices and pharmaceuticals, and agricultural, animal health, chemical and consumer products; sales for 1983: $2.9 billion)

Supervised and coordinated defense of product liability litigation including mass litigation comprising, at any one time, approximately 250 lawsuits.
Counseled divisions with respect to regulatory matters pertaining mostly to the Food and Drug Administration (FDA) and to the EPA, FMC, FTC, ICC, OSHA, and state regulatory agencies. Wrote comments on various proposed regulatory actions.
Drafted various types of agreements.
Provided counsel toward formation of new HomeCare Division.
Reviewed and edited changes to professional labeling ("package inserts") for Pharmaceutical Products Division.
Reviewed and edited advertising for Chemical and Agricultural Products Division and Consumer Products Division.
Recovered over $106,000 in over-assessed freight charges through two actions in the Federal Maritime Commission (FMC).
Monitored and analyzed federal and state legislative and regulatory activities.
Developed document retention policy for Consumer Products Division.
Provided legal counsel to: (a) corporate committee responsible for monitoring work with potentially hazardous biological materials; (b) corporate committee responsible for monitoring work involving recombinant DNA.

**August 1978
to February 1981**

American Society of Hospital Pharmacists (ASHP)   Bethesda, Maryland
STAFF ATTORNEY

(Professional trade association composed of over 18,000 members)

Provided staff and membership with: (a) information on legislative and regulatory programs relating to health issues, particularly drug regulation; (b) legal counsel in areas of antitrust and trade regulation, contracts, copyright law, labor law, and tort law. Obtained income tax exemption for Pennsylvania affiliate of ASHP.

(continued)

EDUCATION

Northeastern University School of Law
    Food and Drug Law Course; Fall Semester, 1982

Villanova University School of Law; J.D., 1978
    Moot Court Society (honorary organization)
    Cited as "best advocate" in Law School Division of American Bar
    Association (LSD/ABA) moot court competition
President of class during first year

Georgetown University; A.B. in Government, 1975
    National Political Science Honor Society

PERSONAL   Member of Illinois and Pennsylvania Bars
                      Interests: basketball, movies, and tennis

REFERENCES   Furnished upon request

John X. Corwin
62 Pine Street
Philadelphia, Pa. 19120

(215) 823-1234

WORK EXPERIENCE:

1978 to
present

United States Attorney's Office
Philadelphia, Pa.
Attorney. Extensive work in anti-trust litigation and motions.

Summer 1977

Silverman and Silverman, Esqs.
Philadelphia, Pa.
Law clerk. Extensive research, case preparation, and client contact in small general practice firm specializing in negligence litigation.

Summer 1976

Redevelopment Authority
New York, N.Y.
Law clerk. Position in the legal division involving research and case preparation in Property and Eminent Domain Law.

January 1975 to
September 1975

O'Shea and O'Shea Assoc., Inc.
New York, N.Y.
Research analyst. Full-time position in an urban consulting firm. Work was primarily with federal and state aid programs for client use as well as the development of housing rehabilitation financing plans.

EDUCATION:

Temple University School of Law
Philadelphia, Pa.
J.D., May 1978

★ Moot Court
★ SBA Orientation Leader
★ Dean's list, spring and fall, 1976
★ Average: B, 3.08

University of Pennsylvania
Philadelphia, Pa.
B.A. in Sociology, December 1974

References available upon request

Edward T. Washington
48-01 129th Street
Philadelphia, Pennsylvania 19137
(215) 675-0121

EMPLOYMENT:

1979 to present

ERA Services, Inc.
Camden, New Jersey

Attorney: Real Estate Department
Professional duties include a wide range of
real estate activities with strong emphasis
in negotiating, structuring, and drafting
agreements dealing with real estate acquisitions,
divestitures, and tax-free exchanges.

1977 - 1979

Law Department, City of Philadelphia
Philadelphia, Pennsylvania

Assistant City Solicitor
Bonds and Contracts Division
Principal duties included negotiation and drafting
of a large variety of agreements, including all
types of supply, service, and sales agreements,
concession contracts, and professional service
agreements. Also involvement in a wide range of
real estate transactions from deed and title problems
to lease negotiations.

EDUCATION:

J.D. Degree, Temple University School of Law - 1976
- Graduated in top third of class
- Participated in several Moot Court trials

B.A., Pennsylvania State University - 1973
- Major in General Arts and Sciences;
  minor in Political Science
- Treasurer and member of fraternity
- Member of Varsity Debating Team
- Dean's List, 1972-1973
- Graduated Cum Laude

**PROFESSIONAL
ACTIVITIES:**

Member of Pennsylvania Bar

References available upon request

ALVARO SUAREZ

40 West 72nd Street
New York, New York   10023

(212)   787-0871

JOB OBJECTIVE

Diversified commercial practice with a primary focus on real estate, financing, and syndication.

EMPLOYMENT

1982 –
present

F.W. Woolworth Co.
Mid-Atlantic Regional Office, Real Estate Department
New York, New York

Attorney.   Duties include all phases of acquisition, disposition, and administration of properties owned or controlled by F.W. Woolworth Co., together with site development and leasing.

EDUCATION

Temple University School of Law
J.D., 1982
Associate Editor, Temple Law Quarterly, 1981–1982

Kalamazoo College, Michigan
B.A., 1979
Passed with distinction the comprehensive examinations in major course of study, Political Science.

AFFILIATIONS AND ASSOCIATIONS

New York Bar Association
Pennsylvania Bar Association
Temple Alumni Association

REFERENCES

Available upon request

LAURIE ADAMS

24 Oak Park Road
Philadelphia, Pennsylvania 19106
(215) 134-4416

Member Pennsylvania Bar
Admitted October 1977

EXPERIENCE:
Feb. 1978
to present

Israel H. Borman, Esquire
Philadelphia, Pennsylvania

ASSOCIATE
General practice - emphasis on negligence work.

Summer 1976

United States Attorney's Office
Philadelphia, Pennsylvania

LAW CLERK

EDUCATION:

Vermont Law School
South Royalton, Vermont
J.D., June 1977

- Member, Vermont Law Review
- Lawyers Cooperative Publishing Company
    American Jurisprudence Book Award for
    Civil Procedure
- Moot Court Competition
- Law School Newspaper

George Washington University
Washington, D.C.
B.A., Political Science, May 1972

- George Washington University Legal Aid Society
- School Newspaper
- Intramural Sports Program

REFERENCES AND
WRITING SAMPLES:

Available upon request.

Hillary Fay
65 Elm Street
Kirkwood, Michigan 48228
(313) 679-2546

LEGAL EXPERIENCE:

March 1984
to present

Howell and Brooks, P.C.
Detroit, Michigan
* Associate
Involved in all aspects of general civil litigation.

June 1983
March 1984

* Research Assistant for Professor Israel Saltman, reporter for Criminal Procedure
  Rules Committee for Supreme Court of Wisconsin
Responsibilities included researching federal rules of criminal procedure,
  comparable ABA guidelines, and Wisconsin cases and statutes.

Summer 1982

U.S. Attorney
Eastern District of Michigan
Detroit, Michigan
* Law Clerk
Responsibilities included writing appellate briefs and motions for dismissal for
  both civil and criminal cases.

LEGAL ACTIVITIES:

Member of Michigan, Federal, and Detroit Bar Associations

EDUCATION:

Michigan University Law School
Detroit, Michigan
Juris Doctor Degree — May 1983
Cumulative Average — 3.0

University of Connecticut
Storrs, Connecticut
Graduate work in Physical Chemistry,

1963 – 1966 (all requirements completed for M.S. except thesis)

HONORS: Research Assistantship and Graduate Teaching Assistantship

American University
Washington, D.C.
B.S. in Chemistry, Cum Laude, 1963

HONORS: Phi Beta Kappa
   Pi Mu Epsilon (Mathematics Honor Society)

OTHER EXPERIENCE:

Chemistry Teacher, 1966 – 1971
Perth Amboy, New Jersey

Fannie Silverman's Day Care Center, 1971 – 1979. Principal organizer, treasurer
  and incorporator

AWARDS:

Honored by the Kiawanis for significant contribution to quality child care in
  Middlesex County, New Jersey, 1977 and 1979.

Honored by the Elks for volunteer work with handicapped children.

Mercer County, Woman of the Year 1975.

References and a legal writing sample will be furnished upon request.

KELLY LEIGH McGEE
Dunsmill Road
Bordentown, N.J. 08505

(609) 297-4141

EMPLOYMENT:

June 1982
to present

Fox, Fox and Frankel, Esquires
Philadelphia, Pennsylvania
Associate, Real Estate Department
Principally deal with commercial sales, leasing, and
financing.

January 1980
to June 1982

Gorman's Inc.
Jensen Beach, Florida
Associate Counsel to ninth largest developer/managers
of shopping centers.

July 1977 to
December 1979

Kongoh and Eckhart, Esquires
Miami, Florida
Associate, Real Estate Department
To a lesser extent, dealt with corporate and commercial
law and franchising transactions.

May 1976 to
July 1977

Hon. Nathan Jones, Court of Common Pleas
Philadelphia, Pennsylvania
Law Clerk
Responsibilities included preparation of memoranda and
research.

EDUCATION:

University of Southern Florida
J.D., 1976

Cum laude
Dean's List 1975 and 1976

LaSalle College
Philadelphia, Pennsylvania
B.A., 1973; Major in Political Science
●Summa cum laude
●Dean's List
●Political Science Award

ADMISSIONS:

Member Pennsylvania Bar - 1976
Member Florida Bar - 1976
Supreme Court of Florida - 1977
Federal District Court for the Southern District
of Florida - 1977

REFERENCES:

Available upon request

DAVID R. CHOSACK
987 Chicago Street
Houston, Texas 77008
(713) 555-1717

EMPLOYMENT

February 1980-
present

Doyle, Dane and Bernback, P.A.
Houston, Texas

Associate, Commercial and Real Estate Department
Duties: Negotiation, preparation, and review of
documents for commercial and residential real estate
transactions; mortgage foreclosures; appearance in
Landlord/Tenant Division of District Court;
representation of major real estate developers before
the Supreme Court of Texas, Superior Court of Texas,
Office of Administrative Law and state, county, and
local land use and environmental agencies.

September 1979-
January 1980

Hon. Samuel Seidman, Appellate Division
Trenton, New Jersey
Law Clerk

Summer 1978

Israel H. Saltman, Esquire
Perth Amboy, New Jersey
Law Clerk

January 1975-
August 1976

Township of Lawrence
Lawrenceville, New Jersey
Township Planner
Duties: Drafting major amendments to municipal
zoning and subdivision ordinances; provide staff
support to local planning and zoning boards.

January--June
and September--
December 1974

Mayor's Office
Boston, Massachusetts
City Hall Intern
Duties: Answering complaints, preliminary interviewing,
research.

EDUCATION

Boston College School of Law
Boston, Massachusetts
J.D., 1979

(continued)

Boston University
Boston, Massachusetts
M.A., 1974; major in Economics and Finance

Boston University
Boston, Massachusetts
B.A., 1973; major in Economics

ADMISSIONS: Supreme Court of Texas
                     New Jersey Supreme Court
                     Massachusetts Supreme Court

REFERENCES: Available on request

Gregory T. Watson
108-43 Homelawn Street
Chicago, Illinois 60632
(312) 771-2257

EXPERIENCE

Friedman and Perch, Esqs., Chicago, Illinois

ASSOCIATE. Responsibility for full range of civil trial and appellate litigation: conduct jury trials; all aspects of discovery; research; writing and argument for motions practice; appellate brief writing and oral argument; pretrial negotiations.

(November 1981 to present)

Illinois Office of the State Appellate Defender

LEGAL INTERN. Assisted the Director by reviewing criminal trial transcripts, substantial research, and brief writing, and counseling incarcerated clients.

(Summer 1980)

EDUCATION

J.D., Georgetown University Law Center, May 1981

Course Concentration: Trial Advocacy
Clinic Participant: Institute for Public Representation
For public interest law firm, monitored client minority and women's groups' efforts to have Equal Employment Opportunity programs established in federal court system; researched corporate democracy and speech issues, drafted comments for filing with Securities and Exchange Commission, and submitted shareholder resolutions relating to disclosure of corporate political activity.

Research Assistant, 1979 to 1981, Institute of Criminal Law and Procedure
Researched and analyzed criminal procedure for federal police/prosecutor relations project, on issues of discretion in arrest and formal charging, and the utility of securing confessions for convictions.

B.A., American University, May 1978

Major: Interdisciplinary Studies (philosophy, sociology, and government). Research thesis on the role of the public defender in the District of Columbia juvenile court system.

Honors: cum laude
Ethics Award

ADMISSIONS TO PRACTICE

Supreme Court of Illinois (1981)
U.S. District Court for the Northern District of Illinois (1981)

PROFESSIONAL ACTIVITIES

American Bar Association, member
Chicago Bar Association, member
Chicago Volunteer Legal Services Foundation, pro bono attorney

REFERENCES

Available upon request

Teresa Ortega

1852 Palm Springs Blvd.
Tallahassee, Florida   32306
(904) 644-3434

EXPERIENCE:

June 1978 to present	Weaver & Weaver, P.A. Tallahassee, Florida ASSOCIATE Extensive matrimonial work including trials, motions, preparation of pleadings.
June 1977 to June 1978	Rosenthal and Rosenthal, Esquires Tallahassee, Florida LAW CLERK Extensive research and brief preparation in wide-ranging areas of the law.
July 1976 to June 1977	Florida State University Law School PART-TIME RESEARCH ASSISTANT

EDUCATION:

Florida State University Law School
J.D., June 1978

Member University Law Review, July 1976 and March 1977
Appellate Moot Court
Phi Alpha Delta Law Fraternity

Boston College
B.A. cum laude, June 1975; major in Political Science

SPECIAL
QUALIFICATIONS: Speak and read Spanish and French

ADMISSIONS: Member Florida Bar
Member United States District Court for the Northern,
     Middle, and Southern Districts of Florida

REFERENCES: Available upon request

DAVID A. SALTMAN

14 Maple Avenue
East Windsor, New Jersey 08520

Home (609) 448-9021
Work (609) 443-7504

EMPLOYMENT:

Private Practice:

September 1975
to present

Newman, Herman, Saltman, Levitt & Feinson, P.A.
East Windsor, New Jersey

Extensive trial work in criminal, matrimonial, and
negligence areas.

Prosecutor:

September 1973
to August 1975

Special Deputy Attorney General assigned to Mercer
County Prosecutor's Office, New Jersey
Chief of Consumer Fraud Unit
Trial Team Member

Law Instructor:

Mercer County Community College, New Jersey
January 1980 to present
General law review

Middlesex County College, New Jersey
February 1977 to January 1979
Business Law I and II and Criminal Justice I

Hightstown High School, New Jersey
January 1977 to March 1978
Law and the Individual

Trenton State College, New Jersey
1973 and 1974
Business Law I

Law Secretary:
August 1972
to May 1973

Baruch S. Seidman, S.C.J.
Chancery and Appellate Division, New Jersey

EDUCATION:

Dickinson School of Law, Pennsylvania
J.D., June 1972
Activities: Legal Aid Society Teaching program, Trial
Moot Court participant, and Student Bar Association.

New York University School of Law
L.L.M., June 1983 (Criminal Justice)

Rutgers College, New Jersey
A.B., June 1969
Major: Business Administration

(continued)

APPOINTMENTS:

October 1982 to present	Municipal Court Judge, Borough of Spotswood, New Jersey
October 1982 to January 1985	Municipal Court Judge, Borough of Helmetta, New Jersey
January 1979 to January 1982	Municipal Court Prosecutor, Washington Township (Mercer County), New Jersey

AFFILIATIONS:

New Jersey Supreme Court
United States District Court for the District of
  New Jersey
Supreme Court of Florida
United States Court of Appeals for the Third Circuit

PROFESSIONAL ORGANIZATIONS AND ACTIVITIES:

Middlesex County Municipal Judge's Association
Editorial Board New Jersey State Bar Association
  Journal
New Jersey State Bar Association
Mercer County Bar Association
American Arbitration Association

PUBLICATIONS:

List available upon request

REFERENCES:

Furnished upon request

Résumé of
Charles Matison

512 East 90th Street
Apartment 717
New York, N.Y. 10021
Phone: (212) 552-1234

Employment:

GENERAL COUNSEL   November 1981--present
Urban Towers Company
New York, N.Y.
Responsibilities include the conduct of all
    litigation.

ASSOCIATE   June 1977--October 1981
Donald David, P.C.
New York, N.Y.
General civil practice, landlord/tenant,
    real estate.

ASSOCIATE   June 1974--May 1977
American Insurance Association
New York, N.Y.
General corporate practice. Began as
    law clerk in 1973 and became Associate
    6 months later.

Education:

Columbia University School of Law, J.D., 1974
Dean's List
Participant in Moot Court Competition, first year

Columbia University
B.A., June 1971, in History
Honors: Dean's List
Coat of Arms Honorary Society
Award Winner, Outstanding Scholarship and Service
    to the University
President, senior class
Vice-president, freshman class

ADMISSIONS: Admitted to the New York State Bar, March 1975
             Admitted to practice in the Southern, Eastern, and Western
               Districts of New York

References:

Available upon request

Gregory L. Charleston
78 Oaktree Drive
Fort Lee, New Jersey 08576

(201) 799-9834

EMPLOYMENT:

October 1968 to present	*Hughes Aircraft Corp.* Woodbridge, New Jersey Corporate Patent Counsel. Handle all phases of patent and trademark law.
September 1964 to October 1968	*Lenox Company* Perth Amboy, New Jersey General Patent Counsel. Handled all design and technological patents.
November 1960 to September 1964	*Ingersoll-Rand Company* New York, New York Corporate Attorney. Handled all phases of patent law practice and was responsible for the administration and supervision of Phillipsburg, New Jersey, Office of the Patent Department, which employed 7 other patent attorneys, 2 patent agents, 2 patent draftsmen, and 17 secretaries.
October 1954 to November 1960	*Catalpa Corporation* New York, New York Counsel. Handled claims, advised on general legal matters.

EDUCATION:

St. John's University
LLB Degree, 1954

Clarkson College of Technology
Mechanical Engineering Degree 1951

ADMISSIONS:

New York State Court, Appellate Division
United States Supreme Court
United States District Court for the Southern District of
   New York
Court of Customs and Patent Appeals
United States Patent Office
Canadian Patent Office

REFERENCES:

Available upon request

Milton Zucker
68 Old Mill Road
Short Hills, N.J.   08807
(201) 555-1212

OBJECTIVE: A responsible position as Patent Counsel offering
                    challenge and growth potential.

QUALIFICATIONS: Extensive experience in Patent Law and in Engineering,
                    most recently, responsibility for patent matters of
                    major division of the company.

                    - patent status investigations and preparation of
                      patent applications.
                    - infringement and validity studies and patent
                      prosecution and litigation.
                    - patent license preparation and review.

WORK EXPERIENCE: The State Street Company, Fairlawn, N.J.

4/73 to present   Position: Patent Counsel

                    Engaged in infringement and validity analyses; patent
                    status investigations; patent litigation; preparation
                    and prosecution of U.S. patent applications in
                    mechanical, electro-mechanical, and electronic art.

9/69 to 4/73   The Estes Company, Elizabeth, N.J.

                    Position: Patent counsel

9/64 to 6/66   General Electric Company, various locations

                    Position: Engineer

EDUCATION: J.D.. 1969 – Seton Hall University School of Law
                    B.S. Engineering, 1964, New Jersey Institute of Technology

MEMBERSHIPS: New Jersey State Bar
                    New Jersey Federal Bar
                    U.S. Patent Bar
                    American Bar Association
                    American Intellectual Property Law Association
                    New Jersey Patent Law Association

References available upon request

Morris Levine
21 East 51st Street
Lubbock, Texas 79409
(805) 274-6262

EMPLOYMENT:

October 1982
to present   T. Hendricks, C.P.A.
                          Lubbock, Texas 79409

                          Corporate Counsel.
                          Advisor on auditing and international tax matters.

June 1981 to
September 1981   Professor H. Feldman
                          Texas Tech University School of Law
                          Lubbock, Texas 79409

                          Research assistant.
                          Research into local and federal agencies and
                             consumer affairs.

EDUCATION: Texas Tech University School of Law
                          Lubbock, Texas 79409
                          J.D., June 1982

                          Class standing: top 5%

                          Texas Southern University
                          Houston, Texas 77004
                          B.A. 1979, Major in Accounting
                          Pre-Law Society
                          Beta Alpha Psi National
                          Dean's List 1978 and 1979

REFERENCES: Available upon request.

Rose J. Martinson
43 Racine Avenue
Mechanisburg, Pennsylvania 17055
(412) 661-5490

EMPLOYMENT:

August 1984 to present	Assistant District Attorney District Attorney's Office Harrisburg, Pennsylvania

Duties involve the preparation for and trial of cases in the Municipal and Common Pleas Courts on behalf of the Commonwealth of Pennsylvania.

August 1982 to August 1984	Senior Corporate Counsel/Real Estate Pizza King Corporation Pittsburgh, Pennsylvania

Responsibilities included acquisition and disposition of properties used in the construction and operation of Pizza King Restaurants. Complete processing of these acquisitions and dispositions involves title insurance, financing, and engineering matters.

EDUCATION:	Boston College School of Law J.D., 1982
	Haverford College, Pennsylvania B.A., Psychology, 1979
ASSOCIATIONS:	Pennsylvania Bar Association Florida Bar Association American Bar Association National Bar Association Philadelphia Bar Association
REFERENCES:	Available upon request

Richard Aaronson
301 East 83rd Street
New York, New York 10028
(212) 555-1212

Date of Birth: June 16, 1953

PROFESSIONAL EXPERIENCE:

1980-   Queens County District Attorney
present   Flushing, New York

               Assistant District Attorney
                 Trial litigation in major felony cases; extensive
                 motion practice; preparation and investigation of
                 homicides, sex crimes, and economic crimes;
                 vehicular homicide supervisor.

1978-   Silverman and Saltman
1980   New York, New York

               Associate Attorney
                 Civil trial litigations, contract negotiation;
                 antitrust and corporate law; Family Court and
                 marital proceedings; and arbitration.

EDUCATION:

               Loyola University School of Law
               New Orleans, Louisiana
               J.D., 1978

               New York University
               New York, New York
               B.A., 1975; Major in Sociology

BAR ADMISSIONS:

               New York Bar Association
               Florida Bar Association
               United States Supreme Court
               United States District Court
                   Southern District of New York
                   Eastern District of New York
               United States Court of Appeals
                   Sixth Circuit

               References furnished upon request.

DONALD DAVID
501 Oak Lane
Long Beach, California 90808
(213) 702-7171

EMPLOYMENT:

July 1984 to present	Office of Juvenile Justice and Delinquency Prevention, U.S. Department of Justice Long Beach, California 90828

Consultant
Advise department on pending actions and
review all cases involving drugs.

December 1983 to July 1984	Harvard Law School, Center for Criminal Justice Boston, Massachusetts 02156

Consultant
Led a research team investigating
alternatives to incarceration.

May 1982 to November 1983	Brooks, Howell and O'Mara, Esquires San Francisco, California 94112

Summer Associate
Researched issues related to litigation and
real estate. Examined and interpreted
contract clauses.

September 1980 to May 1982	Harvard Legal Aid Bureau Boston, Massachusetts 02168

Law Clerk
Interviewed clients, assessed their needs;
advocated client interest before the
Social Security Administration, Welfare
Department, Veteran's Administration, and
Housing Court.

EDUCATION: HARVARD LAW SCHOOL
J.D., June 1983

Course concentration: Criminal Law and
Procedure. Related courses, trial advocacy,
litigation, and labor law.
Best brief, Moot Court Competition, 1981

(continued)

UNIVERSITY OF SOUTHERN CALIFORNIA
B.A., Magna Cum Laude, June 1980

Dean's List, 1980 and 1981
President's award, 1980
Sigma Delta Pi

ADMISSIONS: Member California Bar
                     Member Massachusetts Bar
                     Member New York Bar

REFERENCES: Available upon request

DAVID HERSHFIELD
166 Elm Street
Washington, D.C. 20002
(202) 555-6666

EMPLOYMENT HISTORY:

September 1976
to present

U.S. Marine Corps
Washington, D.C.

Prosecutor and Judge Advocate
DUTIES: Handle the prosecution of felonies
committed by Corps members in North America.

Summer 1976

State of New Jersey, Dept. of Law and Public Safety
Trenton, N.J.

Law Clerk
Fulfilled clerk's general duties in civil service
section of the New Jersey Attorney General's Office.

June 1975
to May 1976

Donald Davis, Esquire
New York, N.Y.

Law Clerk
Responsibilities of clerk in general practice firm
with emphasis on commercial transaction, landlord and
tenant litigation, and domestic relations. Supervised
various aspects of legal practice, collection work,
real estate management, tax return preparation, research
and clerical duties.

EDUCATION:

1975 to 1978

Gonzaga University
Spokane, Washington
J.D., June 1975

  *First year Moot Court program
  *Law Review
  *Member of Environmental Law Society
  *Grade point average, 3.7

Yeshiva University
New York, N.Y.
B.A. in English, June 1975

  *Dean's List, 1971-1975
  *English Honor Society, president 1973-1975
  *Varsity Soccer team captain 1971-1975
  *Sigma Tau Delta

ADMISSIONS:

Member Washington, D.C. Bar
U.S. Court of Appeals for the District of Columbia
U.S. Tax Court
U.S. Court of Appeals for the Seventh Circuit
U.S. Court of Claims
U.S. Court of Appeals for the Fifth Circuit

REFERENCES:

Available upon request.

PARALEGAL

Helen O'Sullivan
100 Royal Court
Stamford, Conn. 06981

(203)787-6043 or
(203)961-8200

RÉSUMÉ
Paralegal

CAREER OBJECTIVE:

To further develop my high level of competency in problem solving, research, and writing while contributing to an established law firm.

EDUCATION:

Cornell University, Ithaca, N.Y.
B.A., May 1985
Major: Economics
Minors: Political Science, History
G.P.A. 3.4

University of London, London, England
Semester abroad program (Spring 1984)

Honors and awards: Omicron Delta Epsilon (International Honor Society)
Emerson Scholar
Dean's List (Four Semesters)

RELATED EXPERIENCE:

Intern, House of Representatives, Washington, D.C.
   Analyzed legislation, attended hearings and markup sessions, provided background summaries to legislative staff, answered constituent mail, handled phone requests. (Summer, 1984)

Research Assistant, U.S. Senate, Washington, D.C.
   Examined, read, and applied necessary information to formulate accurate syntheses on issues ranging from international developmental aid to constituent concerns. (Spring, 1984)

Office Assistant, Matthew Jones, Esq., Dover, Conn.
   Attended court sessions, issued subpoenas, performed research, conducted general office duties. (Winter break, 1983 and 1982)

RESEARCH AND WRITING EXPERIENCE:

Senior Thesis: International Oil Supply
Political Science Tutorial: Ireland and England
Assisted in researching and drafting the Constitution for Hall Councils at Cornell University.

ACTIVITIES:

Resident Assistant
Teaching Assistant
Omicron Delta Epsilon
Pre-Law Society
Peer Advisor

REFERENCES:

Available upon request.

JANE ADAM

(305) 965-4893

10 Intracostal Road
Boca Raton, Florida 33448

EXPERIENCE
October 1983 - Present

Martin & Rothman, Miami
LEGAL ASSISTANT

Expertise in Mortgage-backed Securities and Eurodollar Offerings. Participation in all phases of corporate transactions, including revisions to documents, meetings and correspondence with clients, drafting of closing documents, organization and preparation for closings and attention to post-closing matters.

Other responsibilities include preparation of client bills for Managing Partner, Blue Sky research, Investment Advisor and Broker-Dealer registrations and requisite filings with SEC and NASD; miscellaneous work on acquisitions, exchange offers, project financings, and international debt refinancing.

May 1980 - August 1983

Williams, Brown, and Williams, Miami
ASSISTANT

Maintained law library, created and implemented a new filing system for worker compensation files, operated a PABX switchboard (2,000 incoming calls/day) and trained other employees, performed general office services and special projects for Legal Administrator.

EDUCATION

Institute for Paralegal Training, Miami
Corporate Finance & Business Law
Certification of Graduation, September 1983

University of Miami
Bachelor of Applied Science, May 1983
Major: Office Administration

Related courses: Accounting, Economics, Management, Design and Analysis of Office Systems, COBOL and BASIC computer programming languages

ACTIVITIES

Member, YMCA of Greater Miami, currently serving as a member of the Adult Programming Committee

Alpha Omicron Pi National Sorority, elected First Vice President, 1982-1983

Administrative Management Society, Collegiate chapter member 1980-1982

References will be supplied upon request

Elizabeth Matthews
300 Allen Avenue
Pittsburgh, Pa. 15210
(412) 999-1690

OBJECTIVE: To obtain a challenging position as a paralegal which offers the potential for growth in the corporate or legal community.

EXPERIENCE: Baker & Caldwell
6/85 - Pittsburgh, Pa.
present
Assistant

. Input & evaluate TRW Credit Reports
. Enter & Recap new deal sales on Oakleaf computer
. Interview prospective buyers for bank financing of sale
. Spot deals - complete contracts, issue plates & temporary registration

7/84 - Children's World
1/85 Garden City, New York (Part-time)

Administration

. Coordinated & implemented curriculum for children of various ages
. Instructed beginner computer programming
. Supervised assistants in the execution of daily activities

EDUCATION: University of Pennsylvania, Pittsburgh, Pa.
ABA-approved Lawyers Assistant Program - June 1985
Certificate in Generalist Program - Intensive 12-week course including 40 hours each of instruction in Legal Research: Litigation: Corporations Estates, Trusts & Wills: Real Estate & Mortgages: and 20 hours each devoted to Matrimonial Law and Criminal Law.

Barnard College, New York City, New York
Bachelor of Science - Elementary Education - May 1984
Grade Point Average - 3.8 Deans List all semesters
Honors - Magna Cum Laude/Graduate Achievement Award

Nassau Community College
Garden City, New York
Associate in Science - Education - May 1982
Grade Point Average - 3.6 Deans List all semesters
Treasurer of Early Childhood Club/Trustee Scholarship

INTERESTS: Travel (toured 11 European countries), coin collecting, dance and water sports

LICENSE: Notary Public

REFERENCES: Available upon request

JANE COLLINS
10 Intracoastal Road
Boca Raton, Florida 33448
(305) 965-4893

WORK EXPERIENCE:

October 1983
to present

MARTIN & ROTHMAN
Miami, Florida
Legal Assistant

Expertise in Mortgage-Backed Securities and Eurodollar Offerings.

Participation in all phases of corporate transactions including revisions to documents, meetings and correspondence with clients, drafting of closing documents, organization and preparation for closings, and attention to post-closing matters.

Other responsibilities include preparation of client bills for the Managing Partner, Blue Sky research, Investment Advisor and Broker-Dealer registrations and requisite filings with the SEC and NASD, miscellaneous work on acquisitions, exchange offers, project financings, and international debt refinancing.

May 1980
to
August 1982

WILLIAMS, BRIAN & WILLIAMS
Miami, Florida
Assistant

Maintained law library, created and implemented a new filing system for worker compensation files, operated a PABX switchboard (approx. 2,000 incoming calls daily) and trained other employees, performed general office services and special projects for the Legal Administrator.

EDUCATION:

The Institute for Paralegal Training
Miami, Florida
Corporate Finance & Business Law
Certificate of Graduation, September 1983

University of Miami
Miami, Florida
Bachelor of Applied Science, May 1983
Major: Office Administration

Related courses: Accounting, Economics, Management, Design and Analysis of Office Systems, COBOL and BASIC computer programming languages.

ACTIVITIES:

Member, YMCA of Greater Miami, currently serving as a member of the Adult Programming Committee

Alpha Omicron Pi National Sorority 1979-1983, elected Vice President 1982-1983

Administrative Management Society - Collegiate chapter member 1980-1982

References will be supplied upon request

Alfred Fremont
21 Wyngate Rd.
Philadelphia, PA 19112
(215) 822-3046

EXPERIENCE:
January 1984
to present

LEGAL ASSISTANT, Simone, Garrett and Schwab, Philadelphia, PA
Responsibilities include: Assisting partner in the
representation of various excess insurance carriers of
London by monitoring products liability litigation brought
against their domestic Assureds. Manage a team of paralegals
on a large scale litigation matter. Oversee large volumes
of documents; prepare digests of depositions. Present
position includes travel, case management, and extensive
report writing.

May 1983 to
August 1983

SALES CLERK, General Merchandise, Scranton, PA
Responsibilities included opening and closing store,
pricing, and displaying for this privately owned gift
store.

Summers 1979
to 1982

ACCOUNTING ASSISTANT, Barker's Chocolate, Inc., Scranton, PA
Responsibilities included assisting department heads in the
areas of accounting, purchasing, and customer service.

EDUCATION:

The Institute for Paralegal Training, Philadelphia, PA
Litigation Management Course
Certificate of Graduation awarded December 1983

Westchester College, Westchester, PA
B.A. Sociology, Minor in Criminology, May 1983
Honorary Dean's List

ACTIVITIES:

Member of The Philadelphia Council on Foreign Relations;
Kappa Kappa Gamma Social Sorority; The Philadelphia Area
Runners Association; and The Pennsylvania Paralegal
Association.

REFERENCES:

Furnished upon request.

Michael Warren
200 Saylor Drive
Teaneck, N.J. 07142
(201) 963-4434

OBJECTIVE

Position as a legal assistant in a corporation.

EMPLOYMENT

January 1985 –
Present

Haskins and Rogers, New York, N.Y.

Position: Legal Assistant
Experience in real estate syndication, tax and corporate law; Blue Sky filings; establishment and qualification of general and limited partnerships; assist with preparation and drafting of private placement memorandum and other ancillary documents; setting up of and attendance at closings; and frequent contact with clients and governmental agencies.

May 1981 –
January 1985

Mercy Hospital, Teaneck, N.J.

Position: Senior Social Caseworker
Initial interview and evaluation of applicants.
Detailed record keeping and report preparation.
Organization and evaluation of staff responsibilities.
Counseling clients.
In-house staff training and program development.
Annual Budget and Salary reviews.

EDUCATION

Fairleigh Dickinson University, Teaneck, N.J.
(ABA approved)
Diploma in Paralegal Studies, 1984.
Litigation Concentration (GPA 3.7)

University of Connecticut, Storrs, Conn.
Bachelor of Arts, 1980. Dean's List.
Major: Psychology; Minor: Business

REFERENCES

Personal and professional references available upon request.

Thomas Rincones
101 Lake Street
Arlington, Va. 22201
(703) 229-1488

EXPERIENCE:

1976-May 1986 Barth, Ceaser, Majors & Henderson, Washington, D.C.

LEGAL ASSISTANT
- Responsible for orientation and training of new legal assistants.
- Coordinate work assignments with Support Staff.
- Supervised correction of computer data base.
- Summarized, indexed, and edited deposition transcripts.
- Researched projects at the Securities & Exchange Commission Library and the New York Stock Exchange Library.
- Organized seminars for the firm's international business.
- Cite-checked and shepardized cases for legal briefs using a Lexis Computer terminal.
- Designed formats to facilitate categorization of multifarious documents.

1973 - 1976 Banker's Trust Bank, Washington, D.C.

JUNIOR PERSONAL TRUST AND ESTATE ADMINISTRATOR
- Collected and managed the assets of a decedent's estate by paying bills and income taxes, and establishing investment portfolios.

EDUCATION:

1972-1973 Columbia University, New York, N.Y.

Two semesters completed with concentration in American Diplomatic History, International Organization and Political Relations, International Law, and Economics.

1968-1972 American University, Washington, D.C.

B.A. in History, magna cum laude, with departmental honors, May 1972.

ACADEMIC HONORS: Elected to Phi Beta Kappa, Gold Key Honor Society, Who's Who Among Students in American Colleges and Universities, and the General Honors Colloquium.

ACTIVITIES: Secretary of Gold Key Honor Society, Secretary of History Club, member of the House of Representatives of the Student Government Association, member of the International Student Association, vice-president of Pre-Alumni Council, and participant in the Fisk Exchange Student Program at Colby College, Waterville, Maine, 1970.

LANGUAGE: French

References Available Upon Request

Joan Tremont
21 Oliver Street
Kansas City, Missouri 64116

(913) 929-6003

EXPERIENCE: 7/84 - Present	Silver, Jones & North, Kansas City, Mo. Paralegal. Research; deposition abstracting; document management; LEXIS searches; and Shepardizing.
10/83 - 7/84	Jacobs & Jacobs, Kansas City, Mo. Law Library Assistant. Reference work; inter-library loans; LEXIS searches; Shepardizing; and cataloging of books and periodicals.
12/81 - 8/83	U.S. Peace Corps., Colombia Rural Development Extensionist. Taught classes in Agronomy and English. Designed and implemented community potable water systems. Introduced new vegetable crops and the proper use of modern agricultural techniques.
EDUCATION:	University of Missouri, Springfield, Mo. Bachelor's Degree with Honors, June, 1981 Major: American History Minors: Economics and Music Activities: Student Senate Representative; Presidential Advisory Board Member.
LANGUAGE:	Foreigh Service Institute certified level 4, (native) Spanish speaker.
TRAVEL:	Extensive travel throughout Europe, North and South America.
REFERENCES:	Available upon request.

PEARL LANDAU
176 Audubon Street
New York, New York   10056
(212) 787-6195

EXPERIENCE:

June 1983–
Present

Bertram Goldstein, P.C., New York, New York

Law Clerk in bankruptcy practice. Responsibilities include
research of bankruptcy and related matters, writing memos,
drafting of letters and court pleadings.

January 1983–
June 1983

Israel, Krasner and Madison, New York, New York

Law Clerk with general practice firm. Duties included
research, drafting, pleadings for various cases dealing
with Immigration, Negligence, and Contract Law. Handled
court filings and client interviews.

September 1982–
January 1983

Paine Webber Jackson, Curtis & Co., Inc., New York, New York

Assistant Broker. Solicited new accounts for various
municipal and stock funds.

August 1981–
August 1983

Morgan Guaranty Trust Company, New York, New York

Corporate Trust Administrator. Reviewed indentures,
mortgages, and other financing documents for accounts of
$1 million or more. Responsible for payments and investments
on various trust accounts. Reviewed company compliance with
financial trust agreements.

March 1980–
September 1980

Stein and Day Publishers, New York, New York

Publicity Assistant. Organized author tours, wrote press
releases for all major media. Handled daily managerial
functions of the publicity department.

July 1979–
March 1980

John L. Burns, Jr., New York, New York

Personal Aide. Acted as an assistant press secretary for
W.I.S.E. (lobby group). Assisted in the organization and
management of the opening of the Adeline Moses Burns Gallery
at the Fraunces Tavern. Also acted as a political aide on
Mr. Burns' Exploratory Committee for Federal Office.
Responsibilities included all media and public contact
as well as various research projects.

(cont'd)

EDUCATION:

August 1984-   Attending CUNY Law School.
Present   Participant in Law School's Judicial Clinic during Fall
                    Semester of 1985, assigned to the Criminal Justice
                    Institute. Duties included legal research and preparation
                    of written memorandum. In spring of 1985, assigned to
                    Chief Judge Conrad Duberstein of The United States
                    Bankruptcy Court in the Eastern District of New York.
                    Duties included legal research and preparation of
                    written memorandum.

September 1978-   Attended Fordham University.
May 1982   Received B.A. History and Political Science. Honors
                    include Dean's List and graduating cum laude. Campus
                    editor of university-wide newspaper, member of student
                    government, member of College Council and Financial
                    Aid Committee.

                    References available upon request.

Rebecca Nadard
1600 Andrews Ave.
Albany, N.Y. 12210   Telephone: (518) 968-4113

OBJECTIVE: To obtain a position as a paralegal in either a law firm
                    or corporate legal department.

LEGAL
EXPERIENCE:

January 1985 -   Litigation Paralegal.
Present   Cohen, Stern & Green, Esqs., Albany, N.Y.

                    Responsible for all phases of asbestos and toxic waste
                    litigation including drafting of pleadings; interroga-
                    tories and document productions; motion practice; sum-
                    marizing depositions and digesting of medical records;
                    preparation of case profiles.

September 1984   Paralegal Intern.
- January 1985   Spring Lake Legal Aid, Spring Lake, N.Y.

                    Responsible for interviewing of clients and drafting of
                    pleadings in mostly landlord/tenant and matrimonial areas
                    but also small amount of other types of law. Also some
                    legal research and extensive phone work.

Summer 1983   File Clerk.
                    O'Brien & O'Brien, Esqs., Ballston Spa, N.Y.

                    Responsible for all legal files in four-attorney law firm.
                    Also typed pleadings and court documents and performed
                    general office duties.

EDUCATION: B.A. English, 1984
                    Syracuse University, Syracuse, N.Y.

                    Also certification as a Paralegal from their American Bar
                    Association-approved program. Paralegal GPA 3.0. Studies
                    included: Corporations & Partnerships; Family Law; Patent,
                    Trademark & Copyright Law; Business Law. Also completed 24
                    credits in Business courses.

                    President, Paralegal Student Association, 1984.
                    English Club, 1983 & 1984, College Life Union Board.

OTHER
EXPERIENCE: Part-time employment as department store clerk while
                    attending school.

                    Governess, February 1984 to January 1985 for Mr. and Mrs.
                    William Lewis, Albany, N.Y. Responsible for household
                    duties and complete charge of two young children.

REFERENCES: Available upon request.

Edna Soalman
100 Riverview Drive
Chicago, IL 60698
(312) 861-9612

WORK EXPERIENCE

8/84 to
Present

Black, Miller & Black, Chicago, IL
Litigation paralegal. Prepare memorandums, summarize
depositions, shepardize and cite check briefs, conduct
LEXIS searches, update docket sheets, proofread briefs,
serve and file legal papers, conduct various court work.

3/83 to
7/84

Broadlanes Medical Group, Chicago, IL
Administrative assistant. Researched insurance claims,
analyzed patient inquiries. Promoted after three terms
as typist and office clerk.

1/83 to
3/83

Finney & Robertson, Chicago, IL
Librarian and office clerk. Organized all library
materials, conducted patent searches, assisted in
document production.

3/82 to
5/82

City of Chicago Public Defender, Chicago, IL
Assistant, public defender's office. Interviewed
defendants, researched legal briefs, prepared case
summaries for juvenile court lawyers.

9/80 to
12/82

Chicago Dining Association, Chicago, IL
Dining room manager. Supervised six workers on serving
lines and cleaning areas. Promoted to position after
three terms as student maintenance worker.

EDUCATION

University of Chicago, Chicago, IL
Graduated cum laude, class of 1984
B.A., major in Philosophy. G.P.A.: 3.5

REFERENCES

Available upon request.

John Anderson
201 Fulton Street
Minneapolis, Minn.   55406

(612) 413-2522

CAREER OBJECTIVE:

College graduate and holder of paralegal certificate seeks a challenging
position as a Lawyer's Assistant in the legal or corporate community.

EXPERIENCE:

FEBRUARY 1985 TO PRESENT

Abner, Cohen, Eisner & Henderson, Minneapolis, Minn.

Litigation Paralegal in the Securities Department, responsibilities include
setting up and maintaining files, summarizing and indexing documents,
shephardizing and cite checking, trial preparation, filing and service of
papers and LEXIS training.

SUMMER 1983

Minneapolis District Attorney's Office, Minneapolis, Minn.

Intern. Assisted A.D.A.'s and clerks in preparing cases. Checked
information, retrieved files, spoke with witnesses, photocopied information
and observed courtroom procedures.

EDUCATION:

Pace University, New York, N.Y.
ABA Approved Lawyer's Assistant Program. Courses in Litigation and Legal
Research. Studies consisted of gathering information for the client
interview, preparation of motions and pleadings, briefing of cases,
researching and writing legal memoranda. Certificate, December 1984.

Princeton University, Princeton, N.J.
B.A., Political Science. May 1983
Overall Index 3.5 Italian Minor 3.7

AWARDS & HONORS
The Pope Cultural Society Scholarship of Italian.
Fordham University Scholarship.
Dean's List: 1979-1980
              1982-1983

ACTIVITIES
Vice-President (Pre-Law Society)
Member of Pope Cultural Society
Attended Seminars on law-related subjects.

LANGUAGES:

German

REFERENCES:

Full references will be furnished upon request.

Mark Anderson
16 Meadow Lane
Scranton, Pa. 18518

Telephone: (717) 288-4177

PROFESSIONAL OBJECTIVE:

To obtain a position as a legal or administrative assistant in a law firm, corporation, or bank where my education and training can be used effectively.

EMPLOYMENT EXPERIENCE:

January 1985 - Present

Kranitz & Marlin, Scranton, Pa.
Paralegal, Real Estate Department. Responsible for planning and organizing private and corporate real estate transactions, with much liaison and communication between clients and attorneys.

Summers
1984
1985

Hess & Co., Scranton, Pa.
Sales Extra. Country Club Branch. Duties included creating displays, fashion coordinating, customer service, work with buyers, supervising inventory and reception.

Summer
1983

Security Bank, Scranton, Pa.
Receptionist/Page with the International Department. Responsible for delivering messages; some clerical work.

EDUCATION:

Paralegal Institute, Scranton, Pa.
Specialty in corporations with training and experience in legal research and general skills in real estate and probate. Certificate in 1985.

West Chester University, West Chester, Pa.
Bachelor of Arts degree in Political Science, 1985. Special interest in International Law and Anthropology/Psychology.

MEMBERSHIPS:

Alpha Gamma Delta Fraternity: Social-Standards and Chapter Relations Chairman.
Alumni Club of Scranton, Inc.

LANGUAGES:

French (Reading)

TRAVEL:

Extensive travel in Europe and the Caribbean.

OTHER INTERESTS:

Art, design, travel, reading, and tennis.

REFERENCES:

Available upon request.

ADAM STERN

100 Sycamore Lane
Nashville, Tenn. 37204
(615) 595-1309 (home)

(615) 586-7000 (work)

OBJECTIVE:

Experienced holder of ABA-approved trusts and estates paralegal certificate seeks challenging position.

EXPERIENCE:

1984 - Present   Elliot, Elliot & Farber, Nashville, Tenn.
Trusts and Estates Settlement Assistant.
Prepare, analyze and compile data of new estates; transfer securities, brokerage, custody and check accounts for estates and trusts; terminate and distribute assets of accounts; compile and prepare financial statements, fiduciary and personal tax returns; pay estate and trust expenses for new and ongoing accounts; research and interpret pertinent information concerning estates and trusts, court experience.

1983   Burton Advertising Associates, Inc., Nashville, Tenn.
Assistant to Bookkeeper.
Pressured job, involving deadlines, heavy workload, computing payroll for 250 workers weekly from 3 offices, programming mag card, billing and checking balance sheet for taxes paid by employees.

1982   Carnegie Records, Nashville, Tenn.
Administrative Assistant in the Public Relations Department.
Worked with confidential material and gained familiarity with office procedures.

1978-80   Acme's Emporium, Nashville, Tenn.
Clerk.
Worked to finance education while attending classes on a full-time basis. Successfully assumed the responsibilities of cashier, sales and opening and closing of department.

1977-78   IBM, Endicott, Tenn.
Co-op Assistant.
Duties included terminal work, typing, filing, and heavy phone contact.

EDUCATION:

University of Tennessee, Nashville, Tenn.
Lawyers Assistant Program.
Specialization in Trusts and Estates. (ABA approved) December 1983

Richmond College, Richmond, Va
Bachelor of Arts, Sociology, May 1983
Pertinent Course Work: Accounting 1, Statistics, BASIC computer, SPSS Computer.

PERSONAL INTERESTS:

Golf, Running, Sailing, Racquetball, and Reading.

REFERENCES:

Furnished upon request.

Jeffrey Green

30 Broad Street   (404) 874-6825
Atlanta, Ga. 30397   (404) 916-4411

Experience   CALDWELL & WADE, Atlanta, Ga.

9/84 to   Paralegal
9/86   Assisted in detailed analysis of insurance coverage held by
                Smithville, including General Liability, Worker's Compensation
                and Occupational Disease catagories of coverage; categorize
                and index insurance policies for trial use; general legal
                research (LEXIS Data Base); general work on fee applications
                for Smithville case as well as other bankruptcy clients;
                assisted in set-up work for Chapter 7 auction sales; preparation
                of closing materials for secured lending transactions; analyze
                and outline of collateral arrangements in complex financial
                restructuring transactions.

7/83 to
8/84   KRAVITZ, NEWMAN & MOORE, Atlanta, Ga.

                Paralegal
                Assigned to Agent Orange Product Liability Litigation.
                Responsibilities included: categorizing and indexing all
                pleadings and correspondence; organizing voluminous medical
                data of representative plaintiffs for trial; research and
                retrieval of data on computerized document and deposition
                data bases; monitoring due dates of answers to complaints;
                arranging extensions of time with plaintiffs' attorneys;
                worked as part of group of paralegals on Agent Orange jury
                questionnaires.

Education

9/83 to   University of Georgia, Atlanta, Ga.
Present
                Major: Labor-Management Relations. Courses include: National
                Labor Relations Act, Public Sector Labor Relations, Collective
                Bargaining and Arbitration, Business Law, Criminal Law; Law
                of Administrative Agencies.

2/83 to   University of Georgia, Atlanta, Ga.
8/83   ABA-approved program for Paralegal Studies. Awarded certificate
                with honors after completing intensive six-month course of
                study in General Practice with emphasis on such major areas as:
                Wills and Estates, Corporations, Litigation, Real Estate Law,
                Matrimonial Law, Criminal Law; concentration on legal research.

9/81 to   University of Texas, Austin, Tx.
8/82
                Major: Business Management.

References   Furnished upon request.

Jane Spring
62 Johnson Avenue
Silver Spring, MD 20901
(301) 615-2847

OBJECTIVE: Permanent paralegal position with potential for increased
               responsibility and career advancement with a law firm or
               real estate office.

EXPERIENCE:

March 1984   Davis, Landon, Gurley & Hecht, Washington, D.C.
to Present   Paralegal in the Architect & Engineer Department.
               Attend depositions, digest testimony; coordinate document
               productions, exhibit, and document indexes; assist in
               preparing motions; document toxic tort cases on IBM 3081
               computer. LEXIS training, light legal research. Familiar
               with filing procedures in State and Federal Courts.

January 1983   Reeve's Electronics, Inc., Washington, D.C.
to March 1984 High-pressure job involving heavy workload and high volume
               of direct client contact. Duties included, but were not
               limited to, servicing a diverse customer base in the area;
               assembling and routing the delivery and installation of
               telephone and telephone answering equipment; maintained
               inventory and bookkeeping records.

January 1982   Charlie's Cafe, Silver Spring, MD
to December   Managed this cafe with complete charge of all operations
1982   including inventory, bookkeeping, personnel, auditioning,
               and booking entertainment. During this time I implemented
               several operational changes with positive results.

September 1975 9701 - Restaurant Corporation, Betsville, MD
to September   Assisted in managing this restaurant while attending college.
1980   Responsible for all operations including inventory, menus,
               bookkeeping, and personnel.

EDUCATION: American University, Washington, D.C.
               B.A., English, Creative Writing Emphasis, 1981
               A.A.S., Business, 1980

               College Times, Staff Writer, 1980-81
               Serpentine, Poetry Anthology, 1978

LICENSE: Notary Public Commission

REFERENCES: Furnished upon request

<u>RÉSUMÉ</u>

Martha Bender
1600 Nevada Street, N.W.
Washington, D.C. 20006
(202) 929-3006
(202) 787-3400

<u>GOAL:</u>   Seeking a challenging position as a Senior-Level Legal Assistant which provides an opportunity for both greater responsibilities and future advancement.

<u>EXPERIENCE:</u>
October 1984   Morris, Banker, & Rand
to Present   15 State Street
                Washington, D.C.

CORPORATE PARALEGAL: Responsibilities include training and supervising Unit Trust Department Legal Asistants in the preparation of materials for the issuance and sale of Fortune 100 Corporate and Municipal Bond Funds, compliance with relevant SEC and NASD fund regulations (including 1933 and 1940 Act requirements), direction of financial printing, and coordination of closings with key sponsors (Smith Barney, Kidder Peabody, Drexel Burnham) and evaluation services (Moody's, Standard and Poors). Also assist in preparation of other corporate closings including mergers, debt restructuring, reorganization of Limited Partnerships, and stock offerings.

January 1983 to   Estate of Harris Co., Bankruptcy
October 1984   14 Wall Street
                  New York, N.Y.

REAL ESTATE PARALEGAL: Responsibilities included recon ciliation of Real Estate Claims against the Estate, recording monthly progress of claims processing, and discounting leases to determine fair rental value of breach of lease claims. Developed and maintained a series of indexed systems for internal and court-ordered changes and final disposition of these claims. Also assisted in the development and implementation of EDP System to record this information for all claims against the Estate.

<u>EDUCATION:</u>   New York University, New York, N.Y.
                Took several graduate-level courses in Psychology.

                Skidmore College, Saratoga, N.Y.
                B.A. English, Minor: Fine Arts
                HONORS: Dean's List, 1980-82
                ACTIVITIES: Publicity Director for Student Program Board, Activities coordinator for Seminar in Communications, Student Council, Editor of Literary Magazine.

<u>PERSONAL:</u>   Interests include photography, music, and communications design.

<u>REFERENCES:</u>   Furnished upon request.

Stanley Weiss
18 Darean Drive
Los Angeles, Calif. 90413

(213) 842-2424

CAREER OBJECTIVE

A growth position as a legal professional in a corporation, financial institution, or law firm.

EMPLOYMENT HISTORY

TISHER & WHITE, Los Angeles, Calif.   1983-Present

Corporate Paralegal - Gather data for the preparation and filing of reporting documents (Forms 10-K, 10-Q and 8) with the SEC; prepare and file other 34 Act compliance documents (Forms 8A,3 & 4, etc.), state applications for authority to do business, withdrawal, and change of registered agent; maintain minute books; perform general corporate housekeeping.

Assist in the preparation of registration statements and amendments for real estate income funds (limited partnerships) for filing with the SEC and NASD; coordinate closings; assemble Blue Sky materials.

Participate in the preparation of documents in connection with closings of bank loans; coordinate quarterly review of debt compliance; maintain control records of services of the Trustee/Transfer Agent for the company's securities.

SAN DIEGO DAILY, San Diego, Calif.   1969-1983

Positions included Advertising Manager for small local newspaper, and teacher of Spanish and English as a Second Language for local Board of Education.

EDUCATION

University of California, Los Angeles, Calif. - B.A., 1969
Major: Spanish   Minor: Education

Pomona University, Pomona, Calif.
Legal Assistant Program
Certificate in Corporations, August 1983

JAMES MICHAEL SOLOMON

1619 Lexington Avenue, Apt. 19B
New York, New York 10128
Home: (212) 369-2751
Work: (212) 940-7721

JOB OBJECTIVE:

A supervisory position offering increasing responsibility in the area of law firm administration.

RELEVANT WORK
EXPERIENCE:

January 1984 to Present	Paralegal/Case Supervisor. Smith, Collins, Frederick, Clarkson & Cohen, New York, New York. Handle administrative responsibilities including hiring permanent and temporary paralegals, distributing and supervising work, and working in conjunction with other departments such as word processing; prepare billing to clients, communicate with clients, digest depositions, legal research, create trial exhibits, and organize antitrust litigation files specifically organizing, categorizing, and cataloging large document productions.
Summers 1979-1983	Work experience includes clerking at various retail establishments (including Montgomery Ward) and a bank; responsibilities included sales, administrative, and office work and collections.
EDUCATION:	New York University, New York, New York School of Continuing Education. Courses completed include Practical Account Management (emphasis on planning, workflow, research, presentations, and client relations); Filmmaking: Techniques and Technology; and Film Production I.
	Adelphi University, Garden City, New York Completed lawyer's assistant program (ABA-approved) in winter of 1983; instruction included drafting and communicative legal techniques and legal research.
	Boston University, Boston, Massachusetts Graduated June 1982, with Bachelor of Arts Degree; Major - English; Minor - Psychology. Courses include Public Speaking, Techniques of Debating, Newswriting and Reporting, and Photography (journalism).
	Extracurricular Activities: Program director and disc jockey at WTBU (university radio station); administration, organization and planning in connection with presidential election campaign; and personal solicitation of funds for various charities.
PERSONAL INTERESTS:	Reading, photography, and various athletic activities.
REFERENCES:	Furnished upon request.

JAMES R. FLICK
275 Broadway, #12E
New York, New York 10013
(212) 431-8734

EXPERIENCE:

9/82 - Present   DAVIS, DUNN, FITZPATRICK & McCLELLAN, New York, New York
                   Assistant Paralegal Supervisor. Direct management and
                   supervision of Litigation Department paralegals (18),
                   and coordinate work flow and case assignments in Super-
                   visor's absence; interview prospective applicants;
                   participate in review process; alleviate emergency situations.

8/77 - 9/82   PRINCETON, ROSE, GETTING, & MENDELSOHN, New York, New York
                   Paralegal. Performed all administrative duties relating
                   to large case maintenance with emphasis on entertainment
                   and labor; hired and supervised support staff; established
                   and maintained index systems; researched and determined
                   factual data; supervised document control and information
                   retrieval; document production; cite checking and shepard-
                   izing; trial preparation and attendance; performed statistical
                   analysis and use of LEXIS.

8/76 - 8/77   NUTTER, McCLENNEN & FISH, Boston, Massachusetts
                   Paralegal. Sole paralegal on products liability case with
                   emphasis on support service through computer terminal
                   operation and data retrieval; established and maintained
                   index systems; drafted pleadings; digested depositions and
                   conducted non-legal research.

EDUCATION:

1976   BOSTON COLLEGE, Boston, Massachusetts
                   Bachelor of Arts
                   Major: Art   Minor: English

MISCELLANEOUS: Have attended the following seminars:

                   PLI: Copyrights
                   FEDAPT: Producing in the Commercial Theatre,
                   Broadway & Off-Broadway

REFERENCES: Furnished upon request.

Writing Your Own Résumé

6

Now you are ready to start writing your own résumé. The following worksheets will help you include all the necessary information and arrange it in a concise, organized manner.

After you have filled out the pertinent sections on the worksheets, you will have gathered all of the essential material for your résumé and will be ready to arrange it in whichever format you have selected.

Complete the following worksheets *carefully*. Be sure all information is correct (re-check your dates), because it will become the heart and soul of your final résumé.

I. Identifying Information:

Name: _____

Address: _____
Street and number, city, state, and zip code.

Home Phone: _____
Include area code.

Business Phone: _____
Include area code.

If business phone is confidential, so state; i.e., Business phone: (212) 555-1280 (confidential).

II. Job Objective:

The job objective is optional, but if used, keep it brief. The only time a job objective MUST be used is if you are changing fields.

_____

_____

_____

_____

III. Résumé Capsule:

The résumé capsule, as with the job objective, may be left out.

_____

_____

_____

_____

_____

_____

IV. Educational History:

List information about your high school.

Dates:
From   To
(year)   (year)

_____

Name of High School:

_____

Address of High School:

_____

Diploma Earned:

_____

_____

_____

Honors:

_____

_____

Special Activities
Worth Mentioning:

_____

_____

_____

V. Employment History:

List in reverse chronological order.

Name of Firm: _____

Address of Firm: _____

_____

_____

Position: _____

Dates:

From   *To*
(mo./yr.)   *(mo./yr.)*

Description of Responsibilities:

_____

_____

_____

_____

_____

_____

_____

_____

_____

Name of Firm: _____

Address of Firm: _____

_____

_____

_____

Dates:

From   *To*
(mo./yr.)   *(mo./yr.)*

Description of Responsibilities:

_____

_____

_____

_____

_____

_____

Name of Company: _____

Address of Company: _____

_____

_____

Job Title: _____

Dates:	Description of Responsibilities:
From *To*	
(mo./yr.) *(mo./yr.)*	

_____ _____

_____

_____

_____

_____

_____

_____

_____

Name of Firm: _____

Address of Firm: _____

_____

_____

Position: _____

Dates: Description of Responsibilities:
From   *To*
(mo./yr.) *(mo./yr.)*

_____   _____

                  _____

                  _____

                  _____

                  _____

                  _____

VI. Personal Information:

Height: _____   Willing to Relocate: _____

Weight: _____   Willing to Travel: _____

Date of Birth: _____   Hobbies or Interests: _____

Marital Status: _____   _____

Military Service   (optional):
From   *To*
(mo./yr.) *(mo./yr.)*

_____   _____

               _____

Arm and Branch of Service:

_____

Highest Rank Achieved:

_____

Service Schools or Special Training:

_____

Languages or any other Special Skills:

_____

VII. References:

Though the names of your references should NEVER be included in your résumé, assemble your data as you prepare your résumé. Have a minimum of three people as references.

NOTE: Give complete address — street and number, city, state, and zip code. Include area code with telephone number.

Name of Reference: _____

Position: _____

Law Firm Affiliation: _____

Law Firm Address: _____

_____

Business Phone and Extension: _____

Name of Reference: _____

Position: _____

Law Firm Affiliation: _____

Law Firm Address: _____

_____

Business Phone and Extension: _____

Name of Reference: _____

Position: _____

Law Firm Affiliation: _____

Law Firm Address: _____

_____

Business Phone and Extension: _____

Name of Reference: _____

Position: _____

Law Firm Affiliation: _____

Law Firm Address: _____

_____

Business Phone and Extension: _____

Name of Reference: _____

Position: _____

Law Firm Affiliation: _____

Law Firm Address: _____

_____

_____

Business Phone and Extension: _____

Name of Reference: _____

Position: _____

Law Firm Affiliation: _____

Law Firm Address: _____

_____

_____

Business Phone and Extension: _____

I. Identifying Information:

Name: _____

Address: _____
Street and number, city, state, and zip code.

Home Phone: _____
Include area code.

Business Phone: _____
Include area code.

If business phone is confidential, so state; i.e., Business phone: (212) 555-1280 (confidential).

II. Job Objective:

The job objective is OPTIONAL. If used, keep it brief. The only time it MUST be used is if you are trying to change careers.

_____

_____

_____

_____

III. Résumé Capsule:

The résumé capsule, as with the job objective, is optional; however, one or the other must be used if you are changing careers.

_____

_____

_____

_____

_____

IV. **Employment History:**

List in reverse chronological order.

Name of Firm: _____

Address of Firm: _____

_____

_____

Job Title: _____

Dates:		**Description of Responsibilities:**
From	*To*	
(mo./yr.)	*(mo./yr.)*	

_____   _____

_____

_____

_____

_____

_____

_____

_____

Name of Law Firm: _____

Address of Law Firm: _____

_____

_____

Job Title: _____

Dates: **Description of Responsibilities:**

From   *To*
(mo./yr.)   *(mo./yr.)*

_____   _____

_____

_____

_____

_____

_____

_____

Name of Law Firm: _____

Address of Law Firm: _____

_____

_____

Job Title: _____

Dates: **Description of Responsibilities:**

From   *To*
(mo./yr.)   *(mo./yr.)*

_____   _____

_____

_____

_____

_____

_____

_____

Name of Law Firm: _____

Address of Law Firm: _____

_____

_____

Job Title: _____

Dates: Description of Responsibilities:

From   *To*
(mo./yr.)   *(mo./yr.)*

_____   _____

_____

_____

_____

_____

V. Educational History:

List your education in reverse chronological order. Your most advanced degree or your most recent education is first. List all pertinent details — dates, degrees earned, educational institutions attended.

Advanced Degree:

Dates: Name of University:

From   *To*
(year)   *(year)*

_____   _____

Address of University:

_____

Degree Earned (or credits earned):

_____

Undergraduate Degree:
_____

Dates: Name of College:
From   *To*
(year)   *(year)*
_____   _____   _____

                          Address of College:

                          _____

                          Degree Earned (or credits earned):

                          _____

                          Major: Minor:

                          _____   _____

VI.   Personal Information:
      _____

      Date of Birth: _____   Willing to Relocate: _____

      Marital Status: _____   Willing to Travel: _____

      Hobbies or Interests: _____

      _____

      Professional Memberships and Affiliations:

      _____

      _____

      _____

      _____

      Publications and Major Achievements:

      _____

      _____

Military Service (optional):

From   *To*
(mo./yr.)   *(mo./yr.)*

_____   _____

_____

Arm and Branch of Service:

_____

Highest Rank Achieved:

_____

Service Schools or Special Training:

_____

Languages or any other Special Skills:

_____

VII. References:

Though the names of your references should NEVER be included in your résumé, assemble your data as you prepare your résumé. Have a minimum of three people as references.

NOTE: Give complete address — street and number, city, state, and zip code. Include area code with telephone number.

Name of Reference: _____

Position: _____

Law Firm Affiliation: _____

Law Firm Address: _____

_____

Business Phone and Extension: _____

Name of Reference: _____

Position: _____

Law Firm Affiliation: _____

Law Firm Address: _____

_____

_____

Business Phone and Extension: _____

Name of Reference: _____

Position: _____

Law Firm Affiliation: _____

Law Firm Address: _____

_____

_____

Business Phone and Extension: _____

Name of Reference: _____

Position: _____

Law Firm Affiliation: _____

Law Firm Address: _____

_____

_____

Business Phone and Extension: _____

Law Firm Address: _____

_____

Business Phone and Extension: _____

Name of Reference: _____

Position: _____

Law Firm Affiliation: _____

Law Firm Address: _____

_____

Business Phone and Extension: _____

For Entry-Level Law Graduates

I. **Identifying Information:**

Name: _____

Address: _____
                    Street and number, city, state, and zip code.

Home Phone: _____
                                Include area code.

Business Phone: _____
                                Include area code.

II. **Job Objective:**

The job objective is optional. If used, keep it brief and be sure that it does not limit your opportunities.

_____

_____

_____

_____

III. **Educational Background:**

Begin with your most advanced degree and, in reverse chronological order, list all degrees and certificates. In listing degrees and certificates, give the name and address of the school along with the dates of attendance.

| **Dates:** | | Name of School (Law School): |
| *From (year)* | *To (year)* | |

Name of School (Law School): _____

Address of School: _____

Degree Earned (or credits earned): _____

Major: _____   Minor: _____

Dates:
(year to year)

Name of School (Undergraduate):

_____   _____

Address of School:

_____

Degree Earned (or credits earned):

_____

Major: Minor:

_____   _____

List all merit scholarships, awards, honors, including dates (Law School):

Scholarships:

_____

Awards:

_____

Honors:

_____

Class Standing or Grade Average (only list if noteworthy):

_____

List Extracurricular Activities, School Organizations, etc.:

_____

_____

_____

_____

_____

_____

List all merit scholarships, awards, honors, including dates (Undergraduate):

Scholarships:

_____

Awards:

_____

Honors:

_____

Class Standing or Grade Average (only list if noteworthy):

_____

List Extracurricular Activities, School Organizations, etc.:

_____

_____

_____

_____

_____

_____

IV. Employment History (summer or part-time jobs)

List in reverse chronological order.

Name of Law Firm: _____

Address of Law Firm: _____

_____

_____

Job Title: _____

Dates: *From* *To* *(mo./yr.)* *(mo./yr.)*	Description of Responsibilities:
_____	_____
	_____
	_____
	_____
	_____
	_____
	_____
	_____
	_____

Name of Law Firm: _____

Address of Law Firm: _____

_____

_____

Job Title: _____

Dates:

From   *To*
(mo./yr.) *(mo./yr.)*

Description of Responsibilities:

_____ _____

_____

_____

_____

_____

_____

Name of Law Firm: _____

Address of Law Firm: _____

_____

_____

Job Title: _____

Dates:

From   *To*
(mo./yr.) *(mo./yr.)*

Description of Responsibilities:

_____ _____

_____

_____

_____

_____

_____

_____

Name of Law Firm: _____

Address of Law Firm: _____

_____

_____

Job Title: _____

Dates:

From   To
(mo./yr.)   (mo./yr.)

Description of Responsibilities:

_____   _____

_____

_____

_____

_____

_____

_____

V.   Other Skills and Abilities:

Languages (indicate degree of fluency — reading, speaking, writing):

_____

_____

_____

_____

Special Interests, Hobbies:

_____

_____

_____

_____ .

VI. Early Background:

This is optional and should be used ONLY if there are factors in your background that are truly pertinent to your possible employment.

_____

_____

_____

_____

VII. References:

Though the names of your references should NEVER be included in your résumé, assemble your data as you prepare your résumé. Have a minimum of three people as references.

NOTE: Give complete address — street and number, city, state, and zip code. Include area code with telephone number.

Name of Reference: _____

Position: _____

Law Firm or Company Affiliation: _____

Law Firm or Company Address: _____

_____

Business Phone and Extension: _____

Name of Reference: _____

Position: _____

Law Firm or Company Affiliation: _____

Law Firm or Company Address: _____

_____

Business Phone and Extension: _____

Name of Reference: _____

Position: _____

Law Firm or Company Affiliation: _____

Law Firm or Company Address: _____

_____

Business Phone and Extension: _____

Name of Reference: _____

Position: _____

Law Firm or Company Affiliation: _____

Law Firm or Company Address: _____

_____

Business Phone and Extension: _____

Name of Reference: _____

Position: _____

Law Firm or Company Affiliation: _____

Law Firm or Company Address: _____

_____

Business Phone and Extension: _____

Name of Reference: _____

Position: _____

Law Firm or Company Affiliation: _____

Law Firm or Company Address: _____

_____

Business Phone and Extension: _____

VIII. **Personal Information:**

Date of Birth: _____   Willing to Relocate: _____

Marital Status: _____   Willing to Travel: _____

Military Service (optional):

From   *To*
(mo./yr.)   *(mo./yr.)*

_____   _____

_____

Arm and Branch of Service:

_____

Highest Rank Achieved:

_____

Service Schools or Special Training:

_____

In Chapter 5, you've seen a great number of sample résumés. One of them may seem best for you. Take your completed worksheets, along with your sample and start writing. Don't be discouraged if the first few attempts are not completely satisfying. It may take several efforts before you complete the résumé that is right.

Possibly you have some other ideas that you would like to work into your résumé. Go ahead; but be sure that you include all the pertinent facts and that you adhere to the basic rules governing presentation and information. Below are some do's and don'ts of résumé writing which you should follow.

- DO make it brief.
- DO include name, address, and phone number in a conspicuous place.
- DO include all college degrees and dates received.
- DO list present work experience first, continuing in reverse chronological order.
- DO list all dates of employment, with no unexplained gaps.
- DO give titles of jobs held and succinct accounts of duties.
- DO list major achievements such as publications and awards.
- DO list special skills and foreign languages in which you are fluent.

- DO NOT detail high school career (except special honors if you are a recent graduate).
- DO NOT give academic standing unless in upper 25 percentile, or grade average unless 3 points out of a possible 4.
- DO NOT list summer jobs unless you are a recent graduate or unless job is relevant to career choice.
- DO NOT include present salary or salary desired.

The finishing touches of any work can make it or break it. Here are some additional tips for making your résumé first-rate.

- Use your typewriter to the fullest. Upper- and lower-case, underlining, tabulator keys for consistent indentation, asterisk key for separating sections, etc.
- Use at least half-inch margins on all four sides.
- Place dates so that they will stand out and can be compared easily.
- Skip a line or double space when changing to new subject in order to emphasize data.
- Check and double check your spelling; if in doubt, refer to a dictionary.
- Avoid abbreviations except for degrees or titles.
- Use a new ribbon in your typewriter; it makes for easier reading and better reproduction.

- Have clean typewriter keys.
- Use good bond or other quality paper.
- Use standard 8½″ x 11″ paper.
- Use a tinted paper, if you like, but stay with pale or pastel colors.
- Have copying done by a professional service and don't scrimp on cost.

On the following pages you will find sample résumé layouts. These are not meant to confine you, but rather to show the variations possible. While the samples are all one page long, if you use two pages, place your work history on one and educational background, personal data, hobbies, and such on the other. Staple the pages together, and on the bottom of the first page place a parenthetical indication that the résumé is continued on another page.

Name
Street Address
City, State, Zip Code

Home Phone #
Business Phone #

Employment History

Job Title

From (date)
To present

Name of Law Firm
Address of Law Firm

Describe duties and responsibilities of job.

Job Title

From (date)
To (date)

Name of Law Firm
Address of Law Firm

Describe duties and responsibilities of job.

Job Title

From (date)
To (date)

Name of Law Firm
Address of Law Firm

Describe duties and responsibilities of job.

Educational History

From (date)
To (date)

Name of College
Address of College
Degree Earned

Personal Data

Hobbies

Born (date)
Marital Status
Number of Children

References: On Request

Name   Date of Birth
Street Address   Marital Status
City, State, Zip Code   Number of Children
Home Phone #
Business Phone #

Employment History
_____

                                    Job Title
                                    _____

From (date)   Name of Law Firm
To present   Address of law Firm

                                    Duties and responsibilities of job.

                                    Job Title
                                    _____

From (date)   Name of Law Firm
To (date)   Address of Law Firm

                                    Duties and responsibilities of job.

Educational History
_____

From (date)   Name of Law School
To (date)   Address of Law School
                                    Graduate Degree

From (date)   Name of College
To (date)   Address of College
                                    Undergraduate Degree

References: Available on Request
_____

Résumé of Qualifications

Name	Birth Date
Street Address	Marital Status
City, State, Zip Code	Number of Children
Home Phone #	
Business Phone #	

Career Objective

To use the experience gained in . . .

Educational History

Name of Law School	From (date)
Address of Law School	To (date)
Advanced Degree	

Name of College	From (date)
Address of College	To (date)
Bachelor's Degree	

Employment History

Job Title

| Name of Law Firm | From (date) |
| Address of Law Firm | To present |

Description of duties and responsibilities in the above company.

Job Title

| Name of Law Firm | From (date) |
| Address of Law Firm | To (date) |

Description of duties and responsibilities in the above company.

Job Title

| Name of Law Firm | From (date) |
| Address of Law Firm | To (date) |

Description of duties and responsibilities in the above company.

References: Available on Request

Resumé of _____ *(name)* _____

Street Address   Date of Birth
City, State, Zip Code   Marital Status
Home Phone #
Business Phone #

Employment History

    Job Title
    Name and Address of Law Firm

    Description of job, giving duties and responsibilities.

                                 From (date) to present

    Job Title
    Name and Address of Law Firm

    Description of job.

                                 From (date) to (date)

Educational History

    Name and Address of College
    Degree Received   From (date) to (date)

Hobbies

References:

    Available on Request

Résumé of:

Name

Street Address   Home Phone #
City, State, Zip Code   Business Phone #

Career Objective	To work as a . . .
Employment History	
From (date) To present	Job Title — Name of Law Firm Address of Law Firm Description of duties and responsibilities in this job.
From (date) To (date)	Job Title — Name of Law Firm Address of Law Firm Description of duties and responsibilities in this job.
From (date) To (date)	Job Title — Name of Law Firm Address of Law Firm Description of duties and responsibilities in this job.
Educational History	Degree — Name of College Address of College
Personal	Date of Birth; Marital Status
References	Furnished on Request

Note that these drafts are solely models. You may wish to make deviations in your own résumé.

WORKSHEET FOR RECENT GRADUATES

Name _____

Street Address _____

City, State, Zip Code _____

Phone Number _____

Education

NOTE: Education is listed in REVERSE chronological order (HIGHEST degree first). If you haven't attended or received a degree from a college, substitute high school.

Date   Name of School _____

Degree Earned   Address of School _____

_____   Degree Earned _____

Date   Name of School _____

Degree Earned   Address of School _____

_____   Degree Earned _____

Dates _____   School Honors _____

Summer Experience

(Optional)   Job Objective _____

_____

NOTE: *Employers are listed in REVERSE chronological order.*

Dates from
(mo./yr. — mo./yr.)

_____ Most recent employer _____

Address of employer _____

Job Title _____

Job Description _____

Dates from
(mo./yr. — mo./yr.)

_____ Next most recent employer _____

Address of employer _____

Job Title _____

Job Description _____

Personal

OPTIONAL

Hobby Information: _____

Personal History: _____

Information about Relocation: _____

Military Service: _____

Birth Date: _____

Marital Status: _____

References upon request.

114

WORKSHEET FOR EXPERIENCED PERSONNEL

Name _____

Street Address _____

City, State, Zip Code _____

Home Phone: _____

Business Phone: _____

Experience

Job Objective _____

_____

Résumé Capsule _____

_____

Personal History _____

_____

NOTE: *Employers are listed in REVERSE chronological order.*

Dates:
From   To
(mo./yr.) (mo./yr.)

_____   Most recent employer _____

Address of employer _____

Job Title _____

Job Description _____

Dates:
From   To
(mo./yr.) (mo./yr.)

_____   Next most recent employer _____

Address of employer _____

Job Title _____

Job Description _____

115

Dates:

From   To
(mo./yr.) (mo./yr.)

_____ Next most recent employer _____

Address of employer _____

Job Title _____

Job Description _____

Dates:

From   To
(mo./yr.) (mo./yr.)

_____ Next most recent employer _____

Address of employer _____

Job Title _____

Job Description _____

Education

NOTE: Education is also listed in REVERSE chronological order (HIGHEST degree first). If you haven't attended and received a degree from a college, substitute high school.

Date   Name of School _____

Degree Earned   Address of School _____

_____ Degree Earned _____

Date   Name of School _____

Degree Earned   Address of School _____

_____ Degree Earned _____

Dates _____   School Honors _____

116

Personal

Hobby Information: _____

Personal History: _____

Publications: _____

Information about Relocation: _____

Military Service: _____

Birth Date: _____

Marital Status: _____

References upon request.

Special Résumés for Special People **7**

For some of us, the sample résumés are not enough. Owing to a variety of reasons, you may not be able to follow the résumés included on pages 24-80, but rather, need to deal with a problem that is unique to your circumstances. This chapter considers some of those special circumstances, whether they be a job problem related to age, a hiring advantage in being a member of a minority group, a decision to change fields or career direction, or perhaps a desire to surge ahead in the corporate world.

For Those Over Fifty

If you are over fifty, there is no successful way of disguising the fact. Many "over-fifties" think that if they omit *all* dates they can evade the issue of age. Unfortunately it doesn't work; the evasion merely emphasizes the fact that something is being hidden.

People in personnel, the résumé readers, tend to react adversely to résumés without dates, often discarding them without giving them proper consideration. To be meaningful, a résumé must be factual. Résumés without dates simply are not informative. They can even be counter-productive by creating the impression that you are much older than you really are, or by leading the reader to think that you are trying to hide a difficult-to-explain time gap.

Some counselors advise older people to use a functional style résumé and omit all dates. But personnel people are not stupid. They are quick to recognize any résumé that tells only half a story, that looks as if it is being purposely evasive, and that is not straightforward. Usually such evasions only signal the very fact you are trying to hide. They waste both the reader's and the writer's time. Unless you are truthful, you may as well not bother to write a résumé.

It really is a pity that so many mature people feel their age is a handicap. Whatever its drawbacks, age also has its advantages. Even if some employers are willing to train an inexperienced young person, others prefer the almost-instant productivity that an experienced, mature person can offer.

Our advice to the "over fifty" is simple: in preparing your résumé, follow your chosen format and put in all the appropriate dates. Be proud of your age and experience. State the facts truthfully and with dignity. Preparing your résumé may take a little longer than it would a younger person, but ultimately you will find a satisfying job. For a sample résumé, see page 126.

For Minorities

Most employers are doing their utmost to avoid hiring practices that could be interpreted as discriminatory. Often, as a result of this, previous employment practices are being reversed, and a member of a minority with a good educational background and/or work history is likely to be given preference.

Nonetheless, I suggest that you try neither to emphasize nor conceal your minority background. Listing it as an item under personal data could work to your disadvantage, as it might appear as defiance. Treat it as a matter of course. If you belong to any organizations or professional societies that would indicate your minority status, list them under the appropriate headings.

For the Returning Housewife

The housewife returning to work, like all other job seekers, must have a résumé. Its general format is the same as any other résumé. And, like any other résumé, it must account for all time, even though ten or fifteen years were spent pursuing the functions and responsibilities of a wife and/or mother.

After the introductory identifying information, state the job objective or career goal, if using. This is followed by the dates that were spent at home. The employment history for that period can mention, as simply as possible, the functions of keeping house and raising children. *It is of extreme importance* to include any volunteer work such as PTA or fund-raising in which you were involved.

Never underestimate the value of your volunteer work. Not only has it helped an important cause, but properly described, it will increase your marketability. The very fact that you have done volunteer work tells a prospective employer much about your abilities and interests.

If you have been an administrator for any non-profit organization, it will be assumed immediately that you can offer the same talents to an employer wanting someone for managerial duties. Only a short time ago, we were asked to recruit a mature person with managerial potential to take on the supervision of a market research group. The person hired would direct a staff of interviewers, interview, and hire new employees for this market research function. The person would have to be well organized and have a background that showed managerial abilities.

Several placement counselors were reading résumés in search of such a person. We were looking for a returnee whose résumé showed extensive volunteer administrative experience. We were aware, of course, that many of the people whose résumés we had rejected might have had such experience, but since the information wasn't indicated we could not ask our client to give them consideration.

Many of the returnees' résumés point out interesting and salable talents acquired in voluntary work. Writing an organization's newsletter, organizing fund-raising events, working with the handicapped, door-to-door soliciting of contributions, and other similar volunteer activities show abilities and talents that are very valuable on the job market.

In reviewing your volunteer experience, as in your employment history, list all activities with dates. If you were responsible for any special projects, describe them with the importance they deserve.

Even though fifteen years may have elapsed, your past employment history should be noted. Give dates, job titles, and responsibilities. List any skills such as stenography, typing, bookkeeping, etc. Even if they are a bit rusty, these skills are very useful to prospective employers.

Your educational history should be included, even though there's been a several years' lapse. If you have received a graduate degree and kept up, through journals or books, with the material in your field, this should be mentioned, too. For a complete sample of a returnee's résumé, see page 127.

A returnee's résumé, like any other, should not be sent out without a covering letter. The covering letter should state clearly that you've made provisions for taking care of the home and of any young children. There is no need to go into detail concerning the nature of those provisions, however. (See the sample on page 136.)

Do not be disheartened. Returnees don't always find work easily. But work *is* available and there are many employers who appreciate the qualities — stability, respect for the work ethic, willingness to accept responsibility — that you can offer. An employer might show some concern about the seriousness of your intentions to remain at work, but these doubts are only dispelled after you've made a good impression. In addition, you must recognize that employers often look for what they consider the most gentle way of refusing to hire someone. They are liable to think it is more brutal to say, "I'm sorry, but you don't have what we're looking for," than to tell you, "We'd like to hire you, but we're afraid you'll be concentrating on your home rather than the job."

You are entitled to your privacy, but an employer's concerns sometimes conflict with right. A married man with three children is not questioned about the care of the children. Nor is he asked whether he would be able to continue working if something should happen (or has happened) to his wife. Habits die hard, unfortunately, and some employers still cling to the belief that a mother with dependent children is an employment risk. Your protestations will be useless.

There is a way, however, of demonstrating that you are not a risk. That is by taking temporary employment before looking for a permanent job. Working as a "temp" for a month or two is an excellent idea for a returnee. It serves a threefold purpose: it gives you time to iron out home problems; it gives you a chance to polish up rusty skills; and it gives you a recent reference, proving that your home doesn't interfere with your job. Not only would you want to be able to put those two or three months of temporary work into your résumé, but you could also mention them in your covering letter — they might be the factor that would tip the scales in your favor.

For the Disabled

Effective and convincing publicity consisting not only of paid advertisements but of news stories as well, has done much to alleviate the problems the disabled had in finding employment. Employers are coming to recognize that many of their fears are not only unjustified, but are demonstrably false. Recent studies have shown that, as a group, disabled people suffer less from absenteeism, are involved in fewer work-related accidents, and are more productive than the average abled worker. Some companies, recognizing the benefits accruing from hiring the handicapped, are modifying their offices and plants to remove physical barriers.

A disabled person's résumé does not differ from another person's résumé. It serves the same function: it is a summary of the educational background and work history of the applicant, listing his or her qualifications and assets. As such, it is not the place to discuss a handicap as a problem or as an impediment to employment. For a sample résumé that might be sent out by a handicapped person, see page 128.

While we do not feel that a handicap should be mentioned in the résumé, we do think it should be briefly discussed in the covering letter. Being straightforward and honest is always the best approach. A personnel director of a large office recently said, "The fewer surprises in an interview, the better." Another personnel director told us. "It's like meeting someone whose résumé fits a job's specification perfectly, and then learning he speaks only Chinese."

Obviously, certain jobs are closed to people with specific handicaps, but there are many positions that any handicapped person can fill. A few years ago, we received a résumé from a woman who recently graduated from Cornell University Law School. It indicated that she had majored in history and minored in English, achieving a 3.54 grade-point average over three years. Her covering letter said that she was deaf, but that she hoped it would not prove too great a liability.

We were impressed by her résumé and we replied, suggesting she come for a screening interview. When she arrived, it was obvious that she was not only intelligent, but that she had a very realistic attitude toward her disability. We had no difficulty whatsoever in placing her as a researcher with a large law firm in New York. The last news we have had from her was that she was a senior associate in charge of research.

Although her deafness would have disqualified her for any position requiring phone work, it was not a liability for one involving proofreading, research, and editing. Keep the duties of the job in mind when writing your covering letter. It should be similar to other covering letters in stating your reasons for applying to that particular company and in indicating those points in your résumé of special interest to that company. Only at the very end would you describe briefly your physical handicap. (See the sample on page 138.)

Remember: In your covering letter, your lead should be your assets —not your disability.

Changing for the Better

At any given moment, someone, somewhere, feels as if he or she is on a treadmill going nowhere, and is pondering a radical change of career. Someone else, either laid-off or phased-out, feels that the answer to his or her employment problems is in a field different from the previous one. Whatever the reason, be it choice or necessity, the techniques of a career change are much the same.

The decision should not be capricious. You have to give serious consideration to your prospects, and make an honest evaluation of your abilities and talents before you can even attempt to change your career. You will have to read your résumé carefully and note which of your skills, interests, and previous responsibilities are appropriate to other fields. You are planning to exchange the commitment and expertise you have acquired in one area for the opportunity to prove your abilities in a new field.

We have often seen an attorney become an editor, an engineer become a sales manager, and an executive secretary become an administrator. Teachers usually have a talent for personnel counseling; journalists have much to offer a corporate public relations department; and architects can become superlative display designers. Adele's agency has placed an ex-pilot in a sales program and a nun who left the convent in a job counseling program for international exchange students.

Once you have decided to change fields and have picked an appropriate area, you are ready to write your new résumé. While basically the same as for your original field, this new résumé has one important difference. The job objective or career goal is *not* optional; you *must* include it as well as a capsule résumé. In this manner you explain what sort of work you are seeking as well as how your past experience qualifies you for it.

For instance, if your background is as a patent attorney for an engineering firm and you want to change to a career in technical writing, you state your goal in your job objective:

> *Job Objective:* An opportunity as a technical writer who would use the expertise acquired in ten years as a patent attorney with an electrical engineering background.

Follow the career goal with the same information you would have included for your original field. Remember that your new résumé must be truthful as well as logical. Never put anything in your résumé that is not honest. Stay with the truth even if you feel that a small exaggeration or distortion might make you more marketable. Any information that is not true can become a liability. Employers are willing to train you in areas where you are weak, but not if you had claimed strength in that area. Dishonesty is likely to result in your loss of the job.

A law school instructor wishing to start a new career in litigation should write a complete résumé giving the teaching background, but before the work history, insert a combined job objective and capsule résumé.

> *Job Objective:* A career in litigation which would utilize ten years of dealing with students and parents while a law school professor.

An assistant district attorney looking for a career in anti-trust work uses the same format. The combined résumé capsule/job objective might read like this:

> *Job Objective:* A position in an anti-trust firm in which I can utilize extensive trial and courtroom experience stemming from four years as an assistant district attorney in one of the largest district attorney's offices in the country.

We recently interviewed a research specialist who wanted to change his field to land use law. He enjoyed research, but felt that his present work was too restricted and wanted to be more involved with work directly affecting human lives. We discussed his résumé and decided that merely by rewriting his job objective, the résumé he already had prepared would serve his purpose excellently:

> *Job Objective:* To employ in the field of land use law the broad knowledge gained in six years' work in legal research.

Or an editor of a law journal wanting to leave the publishing field:

> *Job Objective:* A position where my background as editor of journals and researching for articles can be used in the area of corporate mergers.

If you are returning from military service, you will need an up-to-date résumé to land a good job.

Your military service should be treated as a period of employment and should occupy the most prominent position on your résumé. If you decide to use a career or job objective, follow it *immediately* with a concise description of your military career. If you do not use a job objective, the description of your military service must contain the following information:

1. Date (year and month) you became associated with the military
2. Date (year and month) you left the military
3. Arm and branch of service
4. The highest rank received and military occupational specialty
5. Any service schools attended
6. Special training
7. Places you were stationed

Use the work sheets provided on pages 82 to 105 and have all your facts absolutely correct before you start writing.

After the summary of your military career, follow one of the general résumé formats on pages 108 to 112 listing, in reverse chronological order, your education and work histories. For example, if you joined the military right after you graduated from college, place your educational summary immediately after the description of your service history. If, however, you were employed before you joined the military service, the description of your work history should follow the data about your military association.

Bear in mind that the duties of military occupational specialty might not be known to a civilian. For instance, many civilians may not be aware that a Company Master Sergeant is primarily a managerial office worker whose major concerns are assignments of duties, maintenance of schedules, and supervision of other office workers such as company clerks, supply sergeants, and supply clerks.

Military experience can easily be translated to administrative or supervisory job opportunities. For a sample returning service person's résumé, see page 129.

For Jumping Salaries and Job Status

Since neither past salaries nor new minimum salaries should be listed in your résumé, a jump in salary must be implied rather than stated. Remember that the purpose of the résumé is to elicit enough interest in you to get an interview. During the interview is when your salary requirements should be discussed.

HOW SHALL I IMPLY I WANT MORE MONEY?

If your résumé shows that you are presently employed, the reader will infer that you are probably interested in a new job because you are looking for a higher salary. If, however, you are looking for an increase in responsibility as well as salary, state that in your job objective.

For example, if you are an Assistant Public Defender and are seeking a new position as Public Defender, your new goal should appear in the job objective and your present (or past) job title should be included in your employment history. For example:

> *Job Objective:* Public Defender
> (Present or last employment): Assistant Public Defender

When looking for a higher (or different) level, you *must* use a job objective because it is the only way to explain what you are looking for and why you are qualified for such a position. For a typical résumé, see page 130.

"Promotion" Résumés

It often happens that a person has held only one or two positions during a long course of employment, but that within those positions he or she has shown great advancement. In cases such as this, you will document your movement up the ladder with a particular company, rather than show advancement through moves from company to company.

A résumé depicting your job career in one particular company can be very effective if done correctly. Suppose you've been employed for ten years with the firm of Jones and Barney. You started in 1966 as a law clerk; two years later (1968), you were promoted to associate; then in 1974 you again received a promotion, this time to your present job as senior assistant in charge of collections.

A very interesting résumé can be written if you examine each job category individually, detailing it with dates, job titles, and descriptions. Your present or last job title is listed first and, in reverse chronological order, each descending position. An example is given on page 131.

John Spring
26 Waverly Place
Hastings, N.Y. 13076

Phone: (914) 261-1234

Career Objective: To secure either a part- or full-time position
                     in order to re-enter the legal field.

Experience

1950-1978   New York Attorney General's Office
                   Albany, New York

                   Deputy Attorney General

                        My duties included two years of research
                        from 1950 to 1952, and twenty-six years of
                        litigation in land use by developers in
                        northern New York, as well as toxic waste
                        litigation.

Education

1947-1950   Dickinson School of Law
                   Carlisle, Pennsylvania
                   J.D. Degree

1943-1947   Rutgers University
                   New Brunswick, New Jersey
                   B.A. Degree

References furnished on request.

Martha Smith Harley
35 Ridge Street
Scarsdale, New York 10583
Home Phone: (914) 723-0012

EMPLOYMENT HISTORY

1960-Present   **Part-time Advisor**
                      Legal Aid Society
                      Trenton, New Jersey

                      Volunteer work while housewife and mother.

1954-1960   **Senior Associate**
                      Saltman & Saltman, Esqs.
                      East Windsor, New Jersey

                      Associate duties included client contact and
                      extensive matrimonial practice; i.e., trials,
                      motions, filing of complaints, and so on.

1948-1954   **Deputy Attorney General**
                      New Jersey Attorney General's Office
                      Trenton, New Jersey

                      Member of trial section. Extensive trial
                      work including actual trials as well as
                      motions, and so on.

EDUCATION

1945-1948   Harvard Law School
                      Cambridge, Massachusetts
                      J.D. Degree
                      Summa Cum Laude

1941-1945   University of Pennsylvania
                      Philadelphia, Pennsylvania
                      B.A. Degree, Major in Political Science

REFERENCES   Available upon request

NOTE: Nothing should appear on the resumé about the handicap, but it should be mentioned in the covering letter.

Dorothy Rogers
36 Washington Place
Washington, D.C. 20003

Home Phone: (202) 456-1324

EMPLOYMENT:

1972 to present	Veteran's Administration Office of Legal Affairs Washington, D.C. 20010

Attorney
Research and preparation for legislation concerning disabled veterans. Preparation of newsletter to disabled veterans concerning their rights under recently passed or pending legislation.

Summer 1970 and 1971	Saltman & Saltman, Esquires East Windsor, New Jersey

Summer Associate
Research and brief preparation under the direction of Israel H. Saltman, Esquire.

EDUCATION:

Yale University Law School
New Haven, Conn.

J.D. Degree 1972
Graduated with Honors. Average 3.6

Cornell University
Ithaca, New York

B.A. Degree 1969
Graduated with Honors. Average 3.4
Major: History
Minor: English

Extracurricular
Activities: Yale Law Review, Note Editor 1970-1972

Personal
Data: Born: 7/2/59
Marital Status: Single

References will be provided on request.

EUGENE RAFFERTY
300 North Riverside Drive
Nashville, Tennessee 23456
(615) 753-1234

Job Objective: To secure a Senior Associates position with a large
                 law firm.

Military
Service:

June 1973 -   <u>Captain in U.S. Army's Adjunct General's Office</u>
June 1985
                 Stationed in Washington, D.C. Charged with the pro-
                 secution of criminal offences by military personnel
                 throughout army bases in southeastern United States.
                 Honorably discharged.

Education:

1970-1973   UCLA Law School
                 Los Angeles, California

                 J.D. Degree 1973
                 Cum Laude

1965-1969   University of Pennsylvania
                 Philadelphia, Pennsylvania

                 B.S. Degree in Economics
                 Cum Laude

Personal
Data: Born 2/2/46
                 Marital Status: Married - 3 children

                 References on request

Thomas Josephs
435 Drew Street
Cleveland, Ohio 44135

Home Phone: (216) 349-4561

Career Objective: Partner in a law firm specializing in tax law

EMPLOYMENT

June 1979 to   Senior Associate
February 1986   Crane & Crane, Esqs.
                      Cleveland, Ohio

                      Assisted in the supervision of six associates,
                      two paralegals. Was involved in civil litigation
                      concerning tax, including administrative hearings
                      before the Internal Revenue Service, and associated
                      administrative courts.

August 1974   Junior Associate
to May 1979   Windsor & Steel, P.A.
                      Cleveland, Ohio

                      Involved with preparing briefs, complaints,
                      and other legal documents concerning tax
                      litigation.

EDUCATION

1973 to 1974   L.L.M. Degree
                      New York University Law School
                      New York, New York

Theresa McGee
43 Clayton Street
East Windsor, N.J. 08520

Home Phone: (609) 446-4004
Business Phone: (609) 446-7404

Job Objective: To continue a legal career in collections.

1973 to present   <u>Senior Associate</u>
O'Connor & Saltman, P.A.
New Brunswick, N.J.

In charge of collections for Chemical Bank
and Chase Manhattan Bank. Developed
working systems for expediting all litigation
and claims. Collections on behalf of banks
were approximately $10 billion.

1971 to 1973   <u>Law Clerk</u> for the Honorable Albert D. Smith
<u>Appellate Division</u>, Superior Court
Trenton, New Jersey

Responsibilities included research, writing, and
conferences with Judge.

1968 to 1971   University of Florida Law School
Gainesville, Florida
J.D. Degree

1964 to 1968   University of New Hampshire
Durham, New Hampshire
B.A. Degree

References furnished on request.

The Covering Letter

8

Enclose a covering letter whenever you send your résumé to a prospective employer. While it rarely gives any information that is not included in your résumé, the letter is an act of courtesy and a sign of a serious and professional approach to job hunting. It gives each employer a feeling of personal attention.

It makes no difference whether you send the résumé in answer to an ad or as part of your direct mail campaign. The covering letter always follows the same simple rules. It should be brief—limited to one page and no more than four paragraphs. Unlike the résumé, it should never be reproduced. It should be neatly typed and conform to the standards of business correspondence.

Whenever possible, address the letter to a particular individual in the firm. If you cannot ascertain the name, address the letter to the partner in charge of hiring, or, by title, to the head of the department that you are hoping to work in. In answering an ad, however, address your letter as the ad indicates. If this is nothing more than a box number, don't try to guess the title of the person who will be seeing your résumé.

The first paragraph of your covering letter should tell why you are writing to that particular firm. If it is in answer to an ad, so state and give the name and date of the publication where the ad appeared. If a friend who is an employee of the firm has suggested you apply, give the name, title or job category, and department where employed. If writing as part of your mail campaign, explain in two or three lines why work with that company interests you.

The following one or two paragraphs should point out salient features of your résumé that could be of interest to your correspondent. These could be items in your educational background or your work history. In certain circumstances, elaborate slightly on one or two details in your résumé. However, whatever is said should be said briefly.

The last paragraph should be a closing, indicating your hope that you have created interest in yourself and suggesting further communication to arrange an interview.

Since your covering letter highlights certain aspects of your résumé, tailor it to stress your most appropriate skills and talents, and gear it to each particular company that will be the recipient of your résumé. Not only does this call immediate attention to your assets, but it *personalizes* the letter. We believe that a covering letter accompanying a résumé gets more attention from recruiters and personnel people than an unaccompanied résumé, so be sure to always use one in your job search. The following are sample covering letters.

29 Ridge Road
Edison, N.J. 08817
April 15, 1986

Box X3349
New York Guardian
749 East 56th Street
New York, N.Y. 10022

Dear Sir:

I am replying to your advertisement of this date offering a position as tax attorney with your firm.

As my résumé demonstrates, I have my L.L.M. in tax and have been working for the Internal Revenue Service for the past six years.

If my background is of use to you, please contact me at your convenience.

I appreciate your consideration.

Very truly yours,

Anthony L. Blake

Encl.

16 Chilton Street
Cleveland, Ohio 44112
May 9, 1986

George Teasdale
Personnel Manager
Green and Richardson, P.A.
452 Sorrent Drive
Teterboro, New Jersey 07725

Dear Mr. Teasdale:

I am replying to your advertisement in the April issue of the
New Jersey Bar News.

While having no specific background in corporate law, I would
like to point out that my work with Johnson and Johnson legal
division consisted primarily of defense of product liability
cases. I believe this would be beneficial to your corporate law
department, despite the fact that it is not exactly the same
type of work.

My résumé also shows, as your ad requested, a heavy background
in tax work prior to my litigation experience.

I would like to speak with you further. I will be in Trenton
for the American Bar Association meeting next month. Could we
arrange an interview for that time?

Thank you for your consideration.

Very truly yours,

John Villiers

John Villiers

Enclosure

320 Garrity Drive
Chicago, Illinois 60625
May 24, 1986

Harry Wilford, Esquire
Hiring Partner
SMITH & JONES, P.A.
Xenobia, Maine 04874

Dear Mr. Wilford:

I am applying for a position in your insurance defense department, as I feel my experience in litigation will be of interest to you.

As my résumé indicates, I held the position of Senior Associate in the litigation department of the firm of Woodbury and Recon, P.A., for six years. In this capacity, I tried a great number of cases for this firm and was highly successful.

I expect to be in the vicinity of Xenobia in the first week of July. Could we arrange for an interview at that time? As I am currently employed, I would appreciate this be kept in confidence for the present time.

Your consideration is greatly appreciated.

Sincerely yours,

Richard Sheldon

Richard Sheldon

Enclosure

474 Hanover Road
Millville, New York 10901
April 4, 1986

Bernice Luddington, Esquire
Abington & Stor, Esquires
1052 Mamaroneck Avenue
White Plains, New York 10603

Dear Ms. Luddington:

The corporate counsel of your Paramus office, William Scott, Esquire, who is a neighbor of mine, has told me that you have an opening for a tax attorney in your White Plains office.

As you can see from my résumé, I have had extensive experience in the field of tax law prior to the birth of my first child. While I have been unable to seek employment in the field for several years, I have kept my hand in, as it were, by constant reading of all the latest cases and, on occasion, do per diem work for a local tax firm.

My youngest child is now in high school and able to take care of herself. In addition, my sister lives nearby and has agreed to take care of any emergency that might arise; so, I will be able to devote myself whole-heartedly to my job.

I would welcome an opportunity to speak with you. Could I call your secretary for an appointment?

Thank you for your consideration.

Sincerely yours,

Margaret Fries

Margaret Fries

Enclosure

19 Wingate Road
Cleveland, Ohio 44110
July 7, 1986

Irene Gaines, Esquire
Hiring Partner
MORGAN, STERN & GAINES, ESQS.
427 Sunset Drive
Cleveland, Ohio 44265

Dear Ms. Gaines:

I am replying to your advertisement for a paralegal which appeared
in the July 5th issue of The Cleveland Star.

As my résumé shows, I have had six years of consistent paralegal
experience from 1976 to 1982 and have always had an interest in
being employed by a corporate law firm.

I have been home for the past four years with my two young children
but feel I am ready to return to the business world.

I have recently employed a "live-in" college student and am
convinced my children and home responsibilities are properly taken
care of.

I would like very much to meet with you and am available at any
time convenient to you.

Very truly yours,

Linda Martin

Linda Martin

Enclosure

14 Riverside Drive
Syracuse, New York 13243
June 15, 1986

William Jacobson, Esquire
HALL & HALL, P.A.
964 West 44th Street
New York, N.Y. 10032

Dear Mr. Jacobson:

As you can see by the enclosed resume, I will be graduating this month from Cornell University Law School and am interested in finding an entry-level position in your law firm.

Though my long-range goals are in the area of publishing, I am completely realistic about the nature of entry-level positions.

I wish to be frank and mention that I have been deaf since birth, though I am adept at both lip reading and sign language.

I expect to be in New York City during the first week of July and will call your office in hope of scheduling an interview.

Looking forward to meeting you, I remain,

Very truly yours,

Martin Donovan

Martin Donovan

Enclosure

Getting to Know Yourself

9

To be successful in your job search, you must know what you are looking for. Knowledge of the job market, an effective résumé, introduction to a superior list of employers — all great assets in any job campaign — will not help you if you are unaware of your real interests and motivations.

It is well worth spending a little time analyzing the inner you — discovering in what situations you are the happiest, just exactly what excites you. Socrates had a point when he said that the basis of wisdom is self-knowledge, and from that awareness all other knowledge can be acquired. Surely it is impossible to understand anything until you understand yourself.

Self-Analysis Quiz

The following are a few questions which, if considered carefully, will give you more insights into your preferences and will help you in career evaluations. A space is provided for your answer to the left of each question.

_____ 1. Are you person- or object-oriented? Are you happiest
   (a) spending an evening with friends?
   (b) working alone doing home improvements, using your computer, quilting, or gardening?

_____ 2. Do you find yourself
   (a) believing in the pursuit of money as an end in itself?
   (b) being seduced by "causes" and setting other objectives ahead of more money?

_____ 3. Are you a person who
   (a) works best under pressure and is happiest when faced with almost insurmountable demands?
   (b) enjoys a steady, quiet, predictable pace?

_____ 4. Are you usually the "life of the party," the person who initiates group activities?
   (a) Yes   (b) No

_____ 5. Are you happiest when you can be of service to others?
   (a) Yes   (b) No

_____ 6. Are you more comfortable when involved with
   (a) measurable facts?
   (b) creative, abstract ideas?

_____ 7. Are you interested in travel — seeing the country, the world?
   (a) Yes   (b) No

AN ANALYSIS OF YOUR ANSWERS

1. If your answer was (a), you should work in a people-oriented field, such as: matrimonial, worker's compensation, administration, negligence, teaching. If your answer was (b) (hobbies you engage in alone), you would probably be happier in a field not involved with one-to-one relationships, such as: research, anti-trust, tax.

2. If your answer was (a), you would be happy in a profit-making business. Your choices include: corporate law or insurance companies. If your answer was (b), you should try for a job in social service, government, foundations, or the health fields.

3. If your answer was (a), you will find plenty of pressure in such fields as service businesses—collection, matrimonial, negligence, worker's compensation, public relations, employment agencies, or sales. Businesses that involve deadlines are journals and book and magazine publishing. For those who chose (b), a quieter, steadier pace may be found in a field such as teaching.

4. If you answered "yes," you probably are an extrovert and would be happiest in matrimonial, worker's compensation, or negligence.

5. If you answered "yes," you probably would be very successful in such fields as public defender or legal aid society work.

6. If your answer was (a), you will be happiest in research or corporate work.

7. If you answered "yes," you might investigate military law or international law.

This short questionnaire is, of course, incomplete but it should give you some direction in your attempt to understand yourself. Careful and honest introspection is necessary, and once you discover what you really want, you will find such knowledge invaluable.

Where Do You Find Work?

10

Look Around You

A job search, like charity, begins at home. Of all the various job sources, the most convenient — and at times, the best — are your relatives, friends, and neighbors. Almost anyone you know may be the lead you've been looking for. So don't keep your job search quiet; let as many people as possible know that you are job hunting.

Don't be embarrassed about spreading the word. Your friends, too, have been in your position and know that any help is welcome. Were the positions reversed and a friend asked you for help, wouldn't you be eager to assist in any way you could?

Often people hear of job openings in their companies before those jobs are advertised or listed with agencies. Not only are they the first to know about the vacancies, but companies tend to give hiring preference to people recommended by their own employees. Even though a "friend at court" is no guarantee of getting the job, it is more likely that you will reach the interview stage.

If you are convinced of the foregoing and believe that someone you know is going to be instrumental in finding you a job, you'll wonder if you shouldn't put off preparing a résumé until it's needed. We agree. Don't go to the trouble and expense of preparing a résumé until it *is* needed, but a résumé *is* needed the moment you decide to look for work. If a friend or relative suggests your name to his company, he or she will say, "I've told them about you and they're interested, but first they want to see a résumé."

Give the people you know copies of your résumé. It helps them in talking about you and, in addition, they can speed up the decision process by handing in the résumé for you.

Classified Ads

Read the ads! There is a wealth of information in the classified columns of your law journal. You may not find the job of your dreams (although you might), but you can learn much about the job market. You will see what kinds of jobs are open and can get an idea about salaries in the various fields. Through the ads you have a means of testing your salary expectations or, for that matter, your job expectations. You can tell whether you are selling yourself short or aiming too high.

When searching the ads, consider all job titles. An opening for a research attorney, for example, may be listed under librarian; a position as counsel to the vice-president could be advertised as an administrative assistant. Don't let the job titles mislead you; read the entire ad. The duties and the qualifications give much more information about the job than its title.

Do not ignore a good opportunity because the job title is not what you might have expected. Read the classified section carefully and respond to every ad that might be possible. Remember, too, that salaries are approximate. Very often jobs are filled at salaries higher or lower than those offered in the ads. Ultimately, salary depends upon the qualifications of the person selected. For this reason, it is advisable to answer all ads (with which your qualifications coincide to some degree) even if the salary offered is in the extreme lower limit of your range. A job listed at $20,000 might be filled eventually at a salary of $23,000 or one advertised as "to $18,000" might only go to $16,000. In addition, a job listed at a salary less than you had anticipated could offer so much growth and opportunity that it might bear investigation.

Since you are looking for the best possible job, explore as many opportunities as possible, present yourself at as many interviews as you can, and learn as much about each job as you are able. Then, after careful consideration of their opportunities, benefits, and ramifications, accept the job that most closely resembles what you are looking for. (We will go into this in much greater detail toward the end of this book.)

Follow the directions in each ad. If a phone number is listed and it is requested that you call for an appointment, do so; don't arrive without warning. Some job seekers think that an unannounced arrival shows great enthusiasm, but it doesn't. What it does is waste both your and the interviewer's time. If a box number is listed, reply by sending your résumé with a covering letter as discussed in Chapter 8.

Don't be discouraged if you don't get immediate results. At times, as much as three months can elapse before you receive a response. Remember that job hunting is harder and more frustrating than working, but once you have had success in your search, the weeks or even months of anxiety and anguish will be forgotten very quickly.

Private Employment Agencies

Consider the services of private employment agencies. Their business consists of finding the right people for jobs and the right jobs for people. They might be able to offer you the help you need. Private agencies recruit and screen applicants for many different firms and, therefore, can introduce you to a number of prospective employers.

Going to an employment agency is equivalent to applying for many job openings at once. The agency can describe every opening it has listed which could be filled by a person with your qualifications and will leave you the choice of which ones you want to investigate further. The agency does your leg work and will keep you informed of new job openings as they arise. Most agencies expect and need résumés, and you should be prepared to give them several copies.

Private agencies charge a fee, which is usually paid by the employer. Be sure that you fully understand what the remuneration agreement is. If you are asked to sign a contract, ascertain precisely what you are committed to before you accept a job. Today it is more customary for the employer to pay the full fee, but some agencies still have jobs listed where the applicant must pay. Some employers may prefer to reimburse the employee for the fee after a certain length of employment. Don't feel embarassed to ask the interviewer at the agency to clarify any questions about the contract. As with any other business arrangement, it is best to have a complete understanding of terms at the very beginning of your relationship.

Finding the appropriate agency is also a very important consideration. Most agencies specialize in certain fields or professions; be sure that the agencies you register with handle your skills or professional qualifications. If you are a patent lawyer, there is no point in registering with an agency or an executive recruiter who specializes in litigation attorneys. Study the agency ads in the classified columns of the periodicals or journals; the types of jobs they advertise will generally indicate their area of specialization.

Since employment agencies are completely involved in recruiting, they can offer advice about current job trends and market conditions. Quite often, too, they assume some of the functions of the trained guidance counselor. Since they are in touch with the current job market, they can see if your particular skills may be appropriate to an industry you never considered.

A few years ago, Adele's agency interviewed a young man who was what is often called over-qualified. He had a Ph.D. in Romance Languages, was completely bilingual in Spanish and English, and had reading and writing ability in French and Italian. He did not want to teach and had followed up what he considered to be every lead for a person of his training—United Nations, foreign embassies and consulates, import-export firms, multi-national corporations, and so on. The offers he received he had refused, since he felt the salaries were completely unrealistic. She agreed with him, but didn't feel she could do anything at the moment for him. His résumé was passed around the office and the law desk called one of her accounts which had a heavy international practice. Unfortunately the applicant needed a law degree to go with the bilingual skills. Three days later, however, the law firm called back suggesting we contact an underwriter at a large marine insurance company. The outcome was that the applicant found a job at the managerial level, with commensurate pay in a field that he had never considered.

For an agency to find a job in this manner is not unusual. Consider your counselor at the agency as your ally. The agency wants to place you in the best available job. If it wants to stay in business, it has to perform. This is also true of executive recruiters, who specialize in high-level placements.

State and Government Employment Agencies

Another fine source of job leads is the state or government employment agency. Unlike private, commercial agencies, government agencies charge no fee to either the job applicant or the employer. Their functions are supported by the government.

If you are serious about your job search, visit your local government employment office. In addition to advising you of job openings in the immediate vicinity, the counselors at these agencies can also give you information on obtaining a government job.

Chamber of Commerce

Your Chamber of Commerce can be extremely helpful in the job search. It can supply you with a list of all of the law firms in your area. Use the list for your direct mail campaign. You might even learn from the Chamber of Commerce of actual job openings and which firms would be most interested in your skills and qualifications.

Government Jobs

Don't overlook the possibilities that government can offer. The U.S. government employs many Americans. One out of six employed persons serves either federal, state, or local governments. The U.S. government agencies such as the United States Attorney's Office, the Federal Court System and the Federal Public Defender hire hundreds of recent law school graduates. Governmental agencies, whether they be federal, state, or local, hire a significant portion of the legal and paralegal work force and, therefore, a government position is a viable option.

The range of job offerings is tremendous. Think of a job classification and rest assured that the government employs people in that category. Many people feel that government jobs still offer the most security, the best health plans, the most liberal vacations, and the most extensive retirement plans.

Should you be interested in government employment, be very methodical in seeking it out. Find out where the openings are now and in the future. No single office takes care of federal, state, county, and municipal employment; each has to be applied for separately.

On the municipal level, call your city or town hall to find out where to go and whom to see. For county employment, another phone call will start the ball rolling. On the state level check the phone book to see if there is a nearby office of the State Civil Service Commission (or Personnel Board). If not, write to the State Civil Service Commission requesting a list of current examinations and job openings. Ask to be put on their regular mailing list, so you will obtain continuous up-to-date information.

The main post office in your town will have some information on examinations and openings in the Federal Civil Service. More complete information may be obtained from the nearest local office of the Federal Civil Service Commission or from the main office in Washington, D.C. Request to be put on the regular mailing list. U.S. government jobs are available abroad as well as within the United States.

If you are interested in government work, stay with it. Read all the literature available — your local library is a fine source. Take all tests for which you are eligible. There are enormous opportunities in government, and it is likely that your perseverance will get you the job you want.

Temporary Services

Temporary services can be extremely useful. Not only are they a means of supporting yourself during your job campaign, but they can even help you in getting the kind of job you really want. They are especially of value to beginners, people in the intermediate level, and those returning to the job market after an absence.

Most job seekers overlook temporary work. They feel that, as their goal is a *permanent* position, they have nothing to gain by taking temporary employment. On the surface this would appear logical, but it does not consider the fact that a temporary position is often the opening wedge of the perfect job opportunity.

Temporary work can usually be obtained by listing yourself for per diem work with the State, County, or local bar journals. It can also be obtained by listing yourself with the legal aid society, public defender's office, and the local lawyer referral service.

In the job search it is always advisable to take any opportunity that lets you get your foot in the door and prove your capabilities. Temporary work also permits you to enlarge your list of contacts by meeting new people. It is not unusual for your supervisor on a temporary job, impressed by your work and learning that you are marking time until you can find a permanent position, to suggest possibilities and leads you wouldn't have found otherwise.

It is important, therefore, to do the best job you can, and to let everyone you meet know that you're looking for a permanent position. You never know who will introduce you to your new employer. Bring copies of your résumé with you and leave one or two with anyone who shows interest.

Another advantage of the temporary services is that they can be extremely helpful to beginners or to persons who are not yet sure where their interests lie. Temporary work lets you experiment, spending a few days in one firm, perhaps a week or so in a court room, or possibly a month with a non-profit organization. It is a way of seeing how each field works and helping you collect information necessary for a wise career choice.

Working on temporary assignments brings no guarantee of a permanent job offer, but there is a guarantee that you'll meet a variety of people, be exposed to many different kinds of businesses, and experience various distinctive working conditions. Most important, you will be gaining additional experience—all of this while getting paid for it! By all means, consider temporary work while on your quest for a permanent job.

Volunteer Work

It may seem strange, but occasionally it can be profitable for you to work for nothing. Volunteer work, like temporary work, is a way of meeting people. The more people you meet, the greater the possibility that someone will point you in the direction of your dream job. Further, volunteer work can help you improve skills for greater remunerative employment.

One of the unexpected delights of volunteer work is that you never know with whom you might be working. Some of those people you see answering the phones on educational television stations during fund-raising campaigns are very high-salaried executives of established companies. One of New York's leading industrial designers spends his Saturdays with three other volunteers at the sales desk of a New York museum. The wife of the owner of one of New York's finest French restaurants spends her Wednesday evenings in the company of ten to twelve other people — most of whom couldn't afford a meal in her husband's establishment — stuffing envelopes for a non-profit organization.

Not only can you meet people who might help you find a job, but at times the volunteer work itself can become a paid position. The woman who directs the display department of a large upstate New York museum first started with them ten years ago when it was only a *small* upstate New York museum. Growing nonprofit organizations often recruit new employees from the ranks of their volunteers.

Even if your volunteer work does not lead, directly or indirectly, to a job, it is a way of filling empty time and can also fill other voids in your life. You meet people who share similar interests as well as people who range across a far wider social and economic scale than you would normally meet. Even if you ignore the fact that you are doing a "good deed," it is not time wasted.

Volunteer work for lawyers or even paralegals is usually easy to find. Your local legal aid society can direct you to an opening to handle some cases. Old agencies or golden age organizations are also sources of work, client contact, and valuable experience.

Direct Mail Campaign

You cannot claim to have done all that is possible to find work if you have not conducted a direct mail campaign. Obviously, your résumé will be an integral part of this campaign so, once you have prepared the best possible résumé, start your campaign.

Compile a list of possible employers. If you want to work where you live or within commuting distance of your home town, the Yellow Pages of your telephone directory is one of your best possible sources. If you are willing to relocate, the reference librarian at the local law library will be an excellent source of information. He or she can refer you to the books you need to compile your list. As a rule, you are not allowed to withdraw these books, but will have to prepare your list in the library's reference room. Since you will probably find you need other information as you go along, this is not a great inconvenience.

The list should not be too long. You don't want to feel that you have involved yourself in an interminable project. Bear in mind that every firm on the list is going to be sent a covering letter with your résumé. You'll need the name and title of the person you plan to write to. Such reference books as *Martindale and Hubbell* can give you this information. Again, the reference librarian will help you.

If you are willing to relocate, do not hesitate to write to firms at a distance from your home. Most firms, when faced with a really "hot" applicant, will either send someone to interview the applicant or pay for the applicant's trip to their main offices. If you are willing to relocate, you should so state on your résumé.

Your covering letter should be brief and written in a conversational tone. Say that you are enclosing your résumé and would like to be considered for a position in that law firm. Also include a short statement indicating why you feel your qualifications will interest the firm. Since you are enclosing a résumé, there is no need to go into detail in your letter.

The letter should never exceed four paragraphs. Your final paragraph should state that you will call in a few days to arrange an interview. *Don't wait for them to call.* The closer you come to personal contact, the closer you are to a job offer.

Type each covering letter individually. Reproduce your résumé, but never your letter. The letter should follow standard business form with sufficient margins, and be attractive and error-free. Remember that the cover letter is your introduction to a prospective employer.

Keeping a Record

Keep a record of each résumé sent and note the dates of your calls and interviews. Also indicate the results of each call and interview, and follow-up with thank-you letters. Don't leave anything to your memory; maintain a written record.

The simplest way of recording your direct mail campaign is to make a carbon copy of the letters as you type them. On the bottom of the carbon, note date and result of your phone call, date of interview, result of interview, and date of follow-up letter. These can be kept in a file folder with a separate sheet — or calendar page — with dates and times of interviews noted. It would be disastrous to set two interviews for the same time.

A second system is to set up a large sheet of paper with column headings across the top. Below are the suggested headings for each column. The headings are separated by vertical lines with horizontal lines to separate the entries. I suggest the following headings:

Résumé Mailing	Follow-Up Phone Call	Interview	Thank-You Letter	Job Offer	Confirmation or "No Thank You, But" Letter
Name	Date	Date	Date	Yes	Date
Title	Results	Time		No	Letter Type
Firm		Interviewer			
Address		Results			
Date Sent					

Note that recording-keeping sheets of this type have been provided on pages 151 through 154 for your convenience.

The third system involves using 4″ × 6″ index cards. Again the information is the same as the other methods. Below is a sample layout for the card:

Mr. Richard Rowe   Mailed 8/1/85
Managing Partner
Lane & Lane, P.A.
424 Park Place
Buford, Pa. 21370

Phone Call: _____
                              (indicate date)

(Note results) _____

Interview: _____
                    (indicate date, time, and interviewer)

(Note results) _____

Thank-You Letter_____
                              (indicate date)

Job Offer _____

Confirmation *or* "No Thank You, But" Letter _____
                                        (indicate date and letter type)

This system is best for a very large mailing. Have the index cards printed up cheaply rather than typing them yourself.

A direct mail campaign is not an inexpensive way of looking for work, but no way really is. Direct mail takes money — for reproduction of résumés, envelopes, postage, and phone calls — and time. But any other method involves as much time. The difference is that the direct mail time is spent in the comfort of your home instead of on buses, on the pavement, and in waiting rooms. If you are pounding the pavements looking for work, you also have expenses for car fare, lunches, and the continual cups of coffee. The job hunt is going to cost you, regardless of how you do it. You've got to spend money in order to earn it.

Résumé Mailing

Name _____

Title _____

Company _____

Address _____

_____

Date Sent _____

Follow-Up Phone Call

Date _____

Results _____

_____

_____

_____

Interview

Date _____

Time _____

Interviewer _____

Results _____

_____

Thank-You Letter

Date _____

_____

Job Offer

Yes _____

No _____

Confirmation or "No Thank You, But" Letter

Date _____

Letter Type _____

_____

Résumé Mailing

Name _____

Title _____

Company _____

Address _____

_____

Date Sent _____

Follow-Up Phone Call

Date _____

Results _____

_____

_____

_____

Interview

Date _____

Time _____

Interviewer _____

Results _____

_____

Thank-You Letter

Date _____

_____

Job Offer

Yes _____

No _____

Confirmation or "No Thank You, But" Letter

Date _____

Letter Type _____

_____

Résumé Mailing

Name _____

Title _____

Company _____

Address _____
_____

Date Sent _____

Follow-Up Phone Call

Date _____

Results _____
_____
_____

Interview

Date _____

Time _____

Interviewer _____

Results _____

Thank-You Letter

Date _____
_____

Job Offer

Yes _____

No _____

Confirmation or "No Thank You, But" Letter

Date _____

Letter Type _____
_____

Résumé Mailing

Name _____

Title _____

Company _____

Address _____
_____

Date Sent _____

Follow-Up Phone Call

Date _____

Results _____
_____
_____

Interview

Date _____

Time _____

Interviewer _____

Results _____

Thank-You Letter

Date _____
_____

Job Offer

Yes _____

No _____

Confirmation or "No Thank You, But" Letter

Date _____

Letter Type _____
_____

Résumé Mailing

Name _____

Title _____

Company _____

Address _____

Date Sent _____

Follow-Up Phone Call

Date _____

Results _____

Interview

Date _____

Time _____

Interviewer _____

Results _____

Thank-You Letter

Date _____

Job Offer

Yes _____

No _____

Confirmation or "No Thank You, But" Letter

Date _____

Letter Type _____

Résumé Mailing

Name _____

Title _____

Company _____

Address _____

Date Sent _____

Follow-Up Phone Call

Date _____

Results _____

Interview

Date _____

Time _____

Interviewer _____

Results _____

Thank-You Letter

Date _____

Job Offer

Yes _____

No _____

Confirmation or "No Thank You, But" Letter

Date _____

Letter Type _____

Résumé Mailing

Name _____

Title _____

Company _____

Address _____

Date Sent _____

Follow-Up Phone Call

Date _____

Results _____

Interview

Date _____

Time _____

Interviewer _____

Results _____

Thank-You Letter

Date _____

Job Offer

Yes _____

No _____

Confirmation or "No Thank You, But" Letter

Date _____

Letter Type _____

Résumé Mailing

Name _____

Title _____

Company _____

Address _____

Date Sent _____

Follow-Up Phone Call

Date _____

Results _____

Interview

Date _____

Time _____

Interviewer _____

Results _____

Thank-You Letter

Date _____

Job Offer

Yes _____

No _____

Confirmation or "No Thank You, But" Letter

Date _____

Letter Type _____

Don't view the initial interview with alarm or fear and trembling. If you find yourself shaking at the prospect of an interview, you have plenty of company. The tens of thousands of people Adele's agency sends out on interviews all have one feature in common: they have fears about being interviewed, and these fears are because they are preoccupied with their weaknesses rather than their strengths.

Trust me. If you examine the interview process, you will see that it loses much of its terror. It is not the ladder up to the guillotine. It is a meeting to amplify the material in your résumé and to inform you in more detail about the job in question. Never forget that the interview is bilateral.

The firm that is interviewing you is just as interested in selling itself to you as you are in selling yourself to them. Your résumé has already done most of the job of selling you. If it hadn't, you wouldn't be at the interview. Very often, after a few questions to clarify or expand upon the details in your résumé, you suddenly find that the interviewer is no longer talking about you, but is telling you of the tremendous advantages of working for that company. You may not realize something that is very clear to us from our perspective — that many a firm has lost an applicant it wanted badly, because the interviewer at one of its competitors described a much more attractive working environment.

You are not present at the interview because the firm wants to torture you. Your presence is a result of someone's feeling that the firm's interests can be served by hiring you. They have, or soon will have, an opening and are trying to get the best person they can to fill it. The information on your résumé has indicated that you *are* qualified; now they are determining if you are the *best* qualified.

With this in mind — that the firm is interested in you — your effort must be directed toward convincing them that *their* best interest lies in hiring *you.* Through your manner you indicate that you are not only the best qualifieb, but that you have assets and abilities that can't display themselves in a résumé. The amplification that the interviewer often seeks is in those intangibles which will ultimately decide whether you and the firm are suitable for one another.

This may seem a strange basis for hiring, but it usually is the decisive factor. When Adele's agency sends a well-qualified applicant out on an interview, it is their practice, if the applicant is not hired, to call the account and find out why they were not satisfied. They do this to learn if there were "holes" in the job specifications, or if the applicant was rejected as a result of details not in the résumé. On occasion they find that there are concrete reasons for the rejection, but it is more common to be told, ". . . not our kind of person," or ". . . wasn't an X employee," or ". . . wouldn't be happy with us." It is futile to try to get more information in these cases. It isn't that the personnel people don't want to tell anything; they themselves can't explain what they *feel* is wrong.

It is difficult to determine what is wrong when the people making the decisions don't know themselves. However, we have come to the conclusion that the three most important intangibles are enthusiasm, sincerity, and honesty.

By enthusiasm, we do not mean a bubbling, ingenuous exuberance. On the other hand, any attempt to be "cool" will be interpreted as boredom, apathy, or antagonism and such attitudes inevitably lead to a rapid, unsatisfactory termination of the interview. Show enthusiasm by manifesting an interest in the job under consideration, in the company offering the job, or even in the interview process itself. Do a little research on the company before the interview. This invariably creates a favorable impression. Furthermore, if the information you obtain on the firm impresses *you* favorably, it has a tendency to "psych you up," to make you *want* to get that particular job, and that, in itself, will come out as enthusiasm as you are interviewed. Much information concerning a law firm and individual lawyers can be obtained from *Martindale and Hubbell*, which is available in almost any law library.

Not only should you avoid trying to be cool, but don't assume any *persona* that is not your own. Few of us have sufficient acting ability to permit us to continue in a role for any length of time, and we would rapidly give ourselves away. Second, no amount of research is going to show you what sort of a person, apart from your qualifications as a worker, the firm is interested in. Even if there is a readily identifiable corporate or real estate image, you have no way of knowing if the image is what they still want.

Be yourself! You'll make the first step toward losing the interview jitters. Knowing that you will be hired for your qualifications and for your personality, *just as they are*, goes a long way toward making you appear an interested and sincere prospect.

Reread your résumé before each interview. Going over your background will help you present yourself as a well-organized person with a calm and positive manner. It is also a means of recalling facts which are not on the résumé but which will probably come up in the interview. These facts will probably include such data as names of supervisors in your earlier jobs and reasons for leaving former (or present) employment. As the interviewers often repeat questions already answered on your résumé or on their application, don't introduce any confusion.

This is also one of the prime reasons for being honest. If you depart from the truth in either your résumé or on the job application, you are putting an additional load on your memory and this will serve only to increase your apprehension. The interviewer expects some nervousness on your part and usually will try to help dispel it. However, if your nervousness increases as the interview continues, it can seem that you are afraid of being trapped in a lie.

Your employment is an inarticulated contract between you and the company. There is a mutual benefit which both parties agree to after assessing the facts available to them. Either party would be justified in cancelling the unspoken contract if the other party had falsified any of the information. If you accepted a job at a low salary scale as a result of a promise of a sizable increase after three months' employment, you would feel that you had been treated unfairly if that raise did not arrive. And your employer is equally justified in cancelling the contract if you had been hired as a result of false information.

Dishonesty is not just a matter of morality. Hiring and "breaking in" a new lawyer or paralegal is an expensive process for a firm. In addition to the clerical costs involved in setting up a new personnel file, adding to the insurance roster, setting up payroll cards, etc., many offices feel that few employees can earn their salaries until they have worked three months. One of the functions of the personnel department of any company is avoiding such unnecessary expenses. Hence, even the suspicion of a lie can keep you from being hired. It is best to be direct, candid, and honest in all your replies.

Many people, for instance, feel that they should exaggerate their previous salaries. Perhaps they feel that they are very well qualified for the $25,000-a-year job, but their previous salary being only $20,000 will count against them; so, they put a little white lie on the application. Yet that may be one of the details that will be checked when calling your previous employer. It is far better to be truthful.

It is possible that your previous employer was known for underpaying employees. It could also be obvious from your résumé that, as your skills and duties with that firm increased over the years, your salary was not increased commensurately. If you feel that the disparity between your previous salary and the one you are seeking is great, explain that the low pay was one of the reasons you left that job.

Another inevitable interview question concerns your reason for leaving previous employment. Here again truth is the only answer. Even if you were dismissed for incompetence, it is wise to say so. It is often obvious from your résumé that you never should have been given the previous job, that you were underqualified for the position. It could be that not you, but the person who hired you, was to blame. Your honesty and candor would bring this out.

Remember that anything can happen *once.* Interviewers start wondering when the unusual happens more than once. It can be accepted that you were fired from one job because your immediate superior ignored Satchel Paige's advice and looked over his shoulder — and saw you gaining on him. People have been fired because their superiors were afraid of the competition. And personnel people know this. *You* become the problem when you give this as the reason for having lost five jobs in two years.

Because anything can happen once, it is possible that you *are* concerned about the reference you would get from a previous employer. This is handled simply. Most people ask if you would mind having any of your former employers called for references. In the event that you are worried about what one of them might say about you, merely tell the interviewer that you would prefer that one of them not be phoned. Explain your reason for believing that you would get an unsatisfactory reference. Once you have brought the matter to light, few personnel people would call to see if there was more to the story than you had divulged. Your candor in this situation serves a double purpose. First, it presents you as a person who is not only straightforward, but realistic. Second, it gives you one less thing to worry about when the interview is over. You don't have the unpleasantness of that previous job lurking in the shadows; it is already in the open.

Even if you don't get the job, don't dismiss the interview as time wasted. If you are a neophyte, at least you gained interview experience. You probably did make a good impression even if your qualifications were not quite what the company wanted. It is also likely that your résumé will be filed and you may be considered for another opening in the near future.

Your appearance at an interview will affect its outcome. Appearance means not only the way you are dressed — which we will talk about shortly — but also the way you communicate non-verbally. You will never have to tell the interviewer that you are nervous in so many words; you will show that by a number of gestures and movements. The nervousness will be understood. The problem will be in restraining those gestures and expressions that show boredom or hostility. While difficult to control, they can be suppressed. Concentrate on the interviewer's words, even to the extent of subvocally repeating to yourself everything that is said. This concentration has a tendency to set up "interference" with the emotional connotation the words might have for you.

Another factor to consider is your actual physical appearance. Overdressing is as great an error as underdressing. The simplest rule to follow is to dress in the same way as you would expect to dress at work if you got the job. With very few exceptions, this means a dark business suit for a lawyer and slightly more casual dress for a paralegal. Your clothes should be neat and clean, and your hair should be so as well. Remember also that you are going to be interviewed by a human being with quirks and prejudices. You do not want to engender instant antagonism by wearing a political button or insignia, or any indication of your views on any controversial subject. We are not suggesting that you have no right to your views, but merely recommending a platform other than a job interview for broadcasting those views.

INTERVIEW DO'S AND DON'TS

There is much else we could tell you, but we feel that if you are intelligent enough to work, you are intelligent enough to know that you shouldn't pick your teeth or clean your fingernails at an interview. Below is a simplified list of the do's and don'ts of the interview.

- DON'T arrange for more than one interview in a morning or afternoon.
- DO be prompt. If for any reason you are delayed, phone and reschedule the interview as soon as you can.
- DO fill out application forms in their entirety even if you are asked for information already on your résumé.
- DO try to appear poised and alert. Make sure your clothing is comfortable, and seat yourself comfortably without sprawling.
- DON'T interview the interviewer. Trying to dominate the interview may give you a feeling of self-assurance, but it won't get you the job.
- DO ask questions. If there are aspects of the job that are not clear, ask. Whether your questions concern duties or benefits, you have a right to know.
- DON'T ask at the first opportunity what the paid holidays and vacations are. You don't want to give the impression that your prime interest is in how little work you will be doing.
- DON'T burden yourself with props. The initial interview is not the place for college credentials, letters of reference, work portfolios, and such, unless you are told to bring them.
- DO be polite at all times. Should the interviewer do anything to provoke your hostility, keep it under wraps until you get out.
- DON'T hide. Some people try to hide their nervousness by hiding parts of themselves. Such mannerisms as covering the mouth while talking or wearing sunglasses indoors are attempts at hiding.
- DON'T be vague. Your answers to all questions should be clear and definite. "I don't know" is often a very good answer to a question.
- DO know what you want. If the interviewer asks, "What kind of work would you like to do for us?" give a concrete answer. "I don't know; I'll do anything," gives the impression that there is nothing you can do.
- DON'T get downhearted. The failure to get a job from an interview doesn't mean that *you* are a failure. There are other jobs and other interviews.
- DO phone back after the interview. You may get the offer at the interview, or it may not come until later. One week after the interview, phone back and ask if you are still "at bat." Keep phoning until you get a definite answer.

Some large corporations hire their lawyers based on skill, aptitude, intelligence, and personality tests. We will say at the outset that we think such tests are sheer nonsense. We are supported by large numbers of psychiatrists and psychologists. We are also opposed by a large number—most of whom earn their living by administering, interpreting, or designing such tests and of whom it may be argued that their opinion is biased.

This is not the place, however, to argue the advantages and disadvantages of testing. They are a fact of life. The best way of handling them is to take them in your stride.

If you have the skills, a test of your skills presents no problem. If you have ten solid years of litigation experience, an aptitude test that shows a deficiency in communication is not likely to affect your employment. An intelligence test is something that may wind up in your personnel folder, but will have little effect on your career. This leaves the personality test.

The personality test can create problems both in being hired and in future work at that firm or corporation. Without a doubt the personality test is the most dubious test of all, but it is the one that the true believers believe in the most. There are serious doubts about the legality of such tests, as they ask extremely personal questions that often have little bearing upon the job in question. Many of the questions bear upon the religious beliefs or sexual attitudes of the testee and often fail to recognize that a test designed thirty years ago may not reflect today's norms. However, until the issue of legality is settled, my advice is to take the test as best you can, keeping in mind two things.

First, beware of all absolute questions that are to be answered with a true or false or a yes or no. You have to consider how a "normal" person would answer. If the question is "Do you *ever* have sexual fantasies?" since most people do at one time or another, the answer is yes. But be careful of something like "Do you *often* have hostile feelings toward your parents?" Read all such questions very carefully, and watch those qualifying adverbs.

Second, keep your eyes open for the same question couched in different words. The designers of the tests expect people to try to "beat" them, and ask the same question in another form. For example, in a yes or no section of such a test, the question, "Do you ever have sexual fantasies?" might appear. Then, later, in a multiple-choice section would appear the question, "How often do you have sexual fantasies?" with a choice of answers among "never—rarely—occasionally—frequently—constantly." A person who might not want to admit to "ever" having such fantasies might be willing, so runs the theory of the test, to answer "rarely" or even "occasionally."

We've already discussed in detail how important a good résumé is, how to go about your job hunt, and how to survive an interview. After the interview, follow up with a phone call or a letter. It is gracious, but can also help get you the job.

Remember your competition. The hiring committee is considering other candidates for the position as well as you. And sometimes it's really a toss-up. A follow-up letter can provide that extra push to get you in the company's door.

THE MAGIC POWER OF ENTHUSIASM

A follow-up letter can help you in competing for a job by providing the magic power of enthusiasm. Employment counselors usually agree that the most enthusiastic person gets the job. So why not provide the enthusiasm? It can only help.

IT PAYS TO SAY "THANK YOU"

The best way to follow up is to say "Thank you." You may want to say it to the person who told you about a job to let the person know that you appreciate the effort, or you may want to thank the interviewer, letting him or her know of your enthusiasm. The letter will keep your image fresh in the person's mind. And that's definitely a plus!

CONFIRMATION COURTESY

Even "after the fact," it pays to follow up. For example, you've been offered a job and have accepted it. But you are presently working and have just given your employer two weeks' notice. A simple confirmation, accepting the job and thanking the person who's hiring you, will reassure your immediate supervisor-to-be that he or she has made the right decision. It may also assure you of a warmer reception two weeks hence when you show up for the first day on the job.

The letter should be simple. Just confirm the fact that you have accepted the job, tell how happy you are to have it, and repeat the date on which you will report to start the job.

"NO THANK YOU, BUT. . ."

You have been offered a job, but for one reason or another you have refused it. It's an awkward situation that can be made smoother by a follow-up letter, especially if you are interested in working for the company at some future time.

Just let them know why you're refusing. Maybe you have accepted another job but are unsure that it will work out satisfactorily. Letting them know will be a way of keeping your options open. If the firm was interested enough to offer you a job at that time, it is quite possible that they will be happy to consider you for a job at some future time, providing the situation is mutually satisfactory. In other words, you are saying, "No thank you, but . . ." Who knows when your letter might pay off in the future? It's apt to make a good impression for your courtesy alone. Companies like to think they are worth your time and effort, especially when they have extended courtesies to you. And, of course, they are worth it!

On the following pages are sample thank-you letters. They are only suggestions, and your particular situation, plus your ingenuity, will dictate exactly what type of letter to write.

May 7, 1986

Richard Trump, Esquire
Hiring Partner
Rockland and Smith, Esqs.
Rockland, Connecticut 06013

Dear Mr. Trump:

I regret that your job offer came a day too late. Just yesterday, I accepted a job as a tax attorney for another firm. I am really sorry because I was impressed with your firm and probably would have fit in very well.

As I am not at all sure how my new job is going to work out, would you please be kind enough to keep my application on file, and contact me if there is another opening in the next few months?

Thank you for your offer, and again, I am sorry I have to refuse it.

Sincerely,

Anne Paulson

Anne Paulson

September 22, 1986

Ms. Joanna Crosley
Hiring Committee
Johnson & Crumpf, P.A.
1435 Commonwealth Avenue
Boston, Massachusetts 02117

Dear Ms. Crosley:

I am delighted to confirm my acceptance of the job as
Senior Litigation Associate. As you already know, I am not
going to report for another two weeks. But I have just given
my present firm two weeks' notice, and will report to you
on October 4th.

Let me reiterate how pleased I am at getting this job.
I was hoping that I would, as I feel that it is the perfect
job for me and I know that I will fit into your company well.

Until October 4th, I am

Sincerely,

Maryann O'Connor

Maryann O'Connor

April 12, 1986

David Jones, Esquire
Smith & Krantz, P.A.
54 Alameda Street
Oakland, California 94610

Dear Mr. Jones:

    I just wanted to write to tell you how pleased I was
to meet with you last Thursday. Thank you for considering me for the position as your assistant. The job is
just what I am looking for, and I think that I would be
able to fit into your company very well.

    Looking forward to hearing from you soon, I am

                          Sincerely,

                          Samuel C. McGee

                          Samuel C. McGee

February 27, 1986

Miss Sandra Morrisey
98 Auburn Street
Brookline, Massachusetts 02145

Dear Sandra:

Thank you for telling me about the job as a Research Assistant with
the firm of Saltman and Saltman, P.A. I have already interviewed
with David A. Saltman, Esq., and I am glad to say that he seemed
impressed with me and that the job is just what I am looking for.

Mr. Saltman will be in touch with me next week with regard to my
job application and my fingers are crossed in hopes of my getting
the job.

In any case, I want to thank you for taking the time to provide me
with this information about a valuable job opportunity. I really
appreciate it.

Regards to your family, especially your sister, Alice, in Maine.

Sincerely,

Kelly

Kelly Leigh McGee

Which Job Do I Take? **12**

You've spent weeks on the hunt and you've bagged your quarry: two or three job offers. Now you have a new problem. Your thoughts change from "How do I get the job I want?" to "Which one shall I accept?" What? You think that's an easy decision and that you'd take the job that offers the most money? Well, maybe yes, and maybe no. There's more to be considered than just money.

Suppose you're a recent law school graduate and you have never worked full time before. You've come to a large metropolis because you know that's where your future lies. You don't know *anybody*. After weeks of searching you have two job offers. In one, the higher paid of the two, you will be working in a small office with one or two other people; in the other, with 5 percent less pay, you'll be a member of a large staff and will have the opportunity to meet lots of people.

Since you've come to the city to start a new life, a job that offers an opportunity to expand your social life might offer something as valuable as money. That is one of the many intangibles in the job selection process. Here are some others:

- Some firms provide training programs; others are willing to pay part (or all) of the costs of specialized courses to add to your skills and knowledge. How valuable is that? What is it worth? What will that additional education be worth in the future?
- Take into consideration the potential in the firm for advancement. How many of the junior associates will advance to senior associates? How many of the senior associates will advance to junior partner? The interviewer should have some type of statistical analysis available for you at the time of the interview.
- Expectations of the firm or company are very important. Does the firm or company expect you to work 60 to 80 hours per week or 40 to 60 hours per week? Do they expect you to handle 300 cases or 10 cases? Is the firm known for hiring young associates and letting them go after they have been "used up"? Consider your objectives and compare them with those of the company or firm interviewing you.
- The geographical location of a job should influence your decision. If it would require you to relocate, should you? Have you thought about the cost of living in a different city? Remember, to judge the worth of your salary properly, it must be compared to the cost of living. What about cultural activities in the new city? And how important are they to you?

- Even without relocation, consider the location of your job. Perhaps you are one of those people who seeks some diversion during the lunch hour — visiting a museum or doing some shopping. A job in the boondocks offering a few dollars more than one close to a cultural or shopping area might not interest you. One requiring fifteen minutes' travel — a short walk from your home — could be preferable to another with a higher salary and an hour's commute. Often, a slight difference in salary is more than eaten up by transportation costs. Besides, time going to and from work is not exactly leisure time!

In making your decision, consider the importance of being happy with your new job. Adele's agency advises entry-level job seekers to take the job they instinctively feel "good" about. We've found that being happy in a job almost guarantees better job performance and hence promotion. We've also found that most companies promote from within and will always consider their staff members for each new job opportunity. Our philosophy is "Proximity is the mother of opportunity," and, therefore, the "wrong job in the right law firm" often or usually becomes the "right job in the right law firm." A beginner should also consider possibilities for future job hunting. Your first job should be considered as a place to learn, to get experience, and to prove yourself.

There are other intangibles to consider. For example, is there a firm cafeteria? Some firms have them and offer good, nutritious food to their employees at low cost. Considering that, in many instances, a full meal at the company cafeteria will cost less than a hamburger and beverage at a luncheonette or fast-food counter, you would be able to save. How important is this in terms of economics and convenience? Certainly worth thinking about!

The health plan offered is another important factor. Young people very often tend to disregard a firm's hospital and major medical plans — they even consider themselves both indestructible and immortal! But anyone, of any age, can suddenly find himself or herself confronted with a stay in the hospital, resulting in large medical bills.

If you are married with children, you probably are more aware of the value of a good medical plan, but do you know that some companies offer psychiatric and dental coverage as well? How many parents of a troubled teenager would welcome psychiatric coverage! Perhaps you have a child who will need orthodontia work in two or three years. If, among your job offers, is a company that offers no dental plan at all and another that offers all or a percentage of dental costs, you must weigh carefully just how important such a plan is to you.

One of the most important factors to consider is eventual partnership. What is the possibility of your becoming a partner? How long will it take you to become a junior partner? How long to become a senior partner? What does a partnership mean? What control will you have of the firm and how much will your vote count?

If you're an "over-fifty" person and expect to stay in this job until your retirement, find out which offer will give you the most career advancement. One of the firms that has offered you a job may have the levels above your position filled by people your age or younger. But another firm might be able to offer you a position as soon as the immediate supervisor reaches retirement age. How quickly can you get promoted? How high can you go in the company? These, too, are considerations.

Just as job searching is a thinking process, so is job selection. There's much to think about in selecting a job. It is never solved by simply flipping a coin. Think about *you*, decide what is important to *you*, and in which job *you* think *your* skills, talents, and abilities will be used to the most advantage, and where *you* will be the happiest.

And once you make the decision, stick to it. Commit yourself. Getting the job is just the first step. The next achievement is to make the job into *your* job. By giving it your all and approaching it with integrity and imagination, you will change your job into a challenging career.